ORGANIZE IT!

ORGANIZE IT!

HOW TO DECLUTTER EVERY NOOK AND CRANNY IN AND OUTSIDE YOUR HOME

MERVYN KAUFMAN

Woman's Day Specials   **filipacchi** publishing

CONTENTS

INTRODUCTION

ARE THE TABLES IN YOUR LIVING ROOM PILED WITH magazines and newspapers you're not quite finished reading but know you will eventually? Are your chairs stacked with books you've convinced yourself you'll find time to enjoy next weekend? Is your home office flooded with bills and receipts that need filing? And are your closets so stuffed—with boxes of family photographs, unfinished baby albums and clothes you never wear, but swear you will one day—that you can't find your shoes in the morning? Do you absolutely hate clutter, but never seem to have enough time or the patience to make a dent in the piles around you? Have you thought about just throwing out the whole mess but can't bring yourself to do it? If this describes you and your home, then this book is for you.

Clutter is a problem we all face in our homes. I know this because every time we ask our readers to tell us what topics they'd like to see covered in the many magazines we produce for Woman's Day Special Interest Publications, clutter-busting ideas, organizing tips and tricks, smart storage solutions and ways to simply find more space are the topics that rise to the top of the list. That's how the idea for this book came about.

Inside, we offer you a room-by-room guide to organizing your whole home once and for all. We start with solutions for entrance halls and mudrooms, move to family rooms and media rooms, and then visit kitchens, laundry rooms, bedrooms, home offices and baths. We also give special organizing attention to closets, attics, basements, garages and even sheds and workshops. Inspirational photographs, advice from top design pros and some of our favorite product ideas are interwoven throughout the chapters.

I hope you enjoy *Organize It!* and I hope it helps you to not only tame but overcome your clutter! And, perhaps, even find your shoes in the morning.

Many thanks to Mervyn Kaufman, a longtime Woman's Day Special Interest Publications writer and resident expert on organization, who wrote and helped compile this book.

Olivia L. Monjo, Editor in Chief,
Woman's Day Special Interest Publications

1 VERY PUBLIC SPACES

WHAT DO YOU CONSIDER the likeliest decorating show-case in your home? Your living room? Dining room? Either may qualify, but don't overlook the foyer or front hall and your back hall or mudroom. In a great many homes, the entrance hall is the first interior space to greet a visitor. In others, of course, it's the mudroom. Either area should be consistently functional, attractive and welcoming, expressing the hospitality that awaits your visitors as well as the style of your home's interior.

Today's living room, which evolved from the traditional parlor—once the center of all home life—tends to be treated formally, a special-occasion place that children and pets are encouraged to avoid. But the dining room has taken on new life—as a part-time library or music room, or a place where youngsters can do crafts and homework. Each space has specific storage needs, for each has a history of attracting clutter.

Illuminated niches behind the sofa (opposite) lend decorating vitality to this living room setting and also create focused locations for displaying collected treasures. Walls and window ledges are clutter-free, and the room has an almost Asian aura of restraint.

FOYER, HALL, MUDROOM

Entrance halls and mudrooms are busy places in any home, no matter what their size or design. Each of these areas is where boots and outerwear are shed, shopping bags and backpacks get dropped, and keys and coins are stashed. Coats, hats, schoolbags, boots and umbrellas are often just left in the open, creating an untidy look.

One way to approach the task of decluttering these busy public spaces is to assume the role of an enlightened guest and pay your home a visit. Enter it as a guest would, through the front door and into the entrance hall, or through a back or service door and into the mudroom. In either instance, what you see should help you decide how to make the space more useful, more gracious and much less cluttered.

FITTING OUT A FOYER. The front hall or foyer provides the basis for a visitor's first impression. If it's cluttered, the impression it makes is murky at best. Keep in mind that a space that's cluttered is usually one that could be put to better use.

The subtly patterned tile floor of this uncluttered entry (top) makes the space look even more ample than it is. Large hooks installed in painted bead board (above) create a highly functional backdrop for a handsome mudroom arrangement. A rich red striped wallpaper envelopes this light-filled foyer (right), which is furnished only enough to make visitors feel comfortable and welcome.

- First, remove everything that isn't nailed down; make each space clean and open so you can assess its potential appropriately.

- Furnish the front hall as you would any other room, but do so sparingly. Instead of a simple table, consider bringing in a small chest or a console table with at least one drawer. Storing items in drawers rather than keeping them out in the open is a sure way to foster an uncluttered look.

- Don't overlook lighting. You don't need to create a blaze of light with high-wattage bulbs or promote a sense of importance with an oversize chandelier. Soft, ambient lighting is what's called for so that guests get a cheery welcome and can see where you want them to put their things.

- Place a small bowl or a basket on that chest or table as a place to put keys and sunglasses, a larger vessel to hold incoming or outgoing mail.

- For the convenience of family members as well as your guests, hang a mirror prominently. That last look, as you're preparing to leave home, is best done just before making an exit.

- Add a coat rack to your entrance hall to relieve the pressure on the guest closet. A tall container for wet umbrellas would be another useful addition.

- Don't clutter your hall with collectibles or family photos. One piece of nicely framed art and a few choice items on a wall-hung shelf can warm the space and make people interested in the particular things you love.

A space-saving mahogany mail organizer (top, left) has two drawers and a divided shelf for books and papers. Handled leather containers on a shelf under an upholstered seat (top) cleverly hide mudroom secrets. Overhead, a Mission-style wall shelf has storage on two levels and hooks sturdy enough to hold heavy winter gear. A sap bucket (above) becomes an eye-catching umbrella stand. Hang your hat or your jacket and tote bag on this handy coat rack (left) with two multi-prong hooks.

END MUDROOM MAYHEM. If, as in most households, your back hall or mudroom is a high-traffic zone, it may tend to be more cluttered than your foyer because it is used so much more.

- Install a bench for putting on and removing boots. It can also be used for storing scarves, galoshes and gloves if the bench happens to include a seat with storage space concealed beneath its pull-up lid.

- Keep pet gear and cleaning supplies out of sight by placing wicker baskets or wood or plastic bins under an open bench.

- Put in a cabinet with open shelves or cubbyholes labeled so each member of the family has a spot in which to stash gear.

- Shop for new or secondhand steel lockers. Painted or left in their natural state, they can provide closed storage for items you don't want displayed.

- Instead of a coat rack, add a series of wall-mounted hooks or pegs to your mudroom, giving anyone entering your house through the back door a spot to hang outerwear.

- Set down a small rubber or plastic mat for muddy shoes and wet boots. A large, flat basket just for shoes would make a decorative alternative.

All of a family's gear and outerwear can be contained in this freestanding organizer (top), which contains four sturdy coat hooks, a bench and two pull-out wicker baskets. An elaborate system of adjustable shelves, combined with a padded bench topping its own storage shelf (above), can put a wall to good use just inside a back door. An elegant addition to a family mudroom (right), this made-to-measure unit has room for storage baskets on several shelves, staggered coat hooks and a long bench, plus under-seat cubbies for shoes, boots and sports gear.

HELP FOR HALL CLOSETS

Closets are integral to both your front and back hall—after entering your home visitors will want to park their jackets. Your job is to create uncluttered spaces that further the spirit of welcome.

- Take everything out; sort the contents as "Essentials," "Store Elsewhere" and "Toss."

- Do a lighting check—and, if possible, an upgrade; change an incandescent to a fluorescent bulb, to spread the light more evenly.

- Return wire hangers to the dry cleaner. Supply a nice set of wooden hangers; make sure they remain there and don't disappear into one of your bedroom closets.

- Stack shelved items neatly or place them in labeled containers. For seasonal items, add "Summer," "Winter," "Fall" or "Spring" to the labels, so the nature of the contents is clearly indicated.

A jam-packed hall or mudroom (above, left) can be organized with the help of vertical storage and handy cubbies. This built-in unit stores shoes, coats, umbrellas and school bags; hooks ensure that everything is hung in its proper place and no space is wasted. Winter boots and blankets can also be neatly tucked away in a storage bin with a lift-up lid (above). Painted white, it can blend with room architecture. When topped with a cushion, it becomes a convenient place to sit when taking shoes off.

Most of the homeowners' collectibles and clutter are contained in a pair of standard-size cabinets that flank the open doorway leading into this living room (above). Books and displayable objects are arranged on open shelving; supplies are kept behind closed doors in the cupboards near the floor. Note that the top molding was a custom addition that mimics the crown molding that wraps around the room.

THE FORMAL WING

Although the traditional living room often receives afterthought status in many of today's new homes, and dining rooms frequently evolve into multiuse rooms or expanded butler's pantries, these spaces continue to hold an honored place in the home. Often there is a tendency to treat them as formal rooms—discouraging most family use except on special occasions—but they both become the workhorse spaces you depend on when you entertain guests or celebrate the holidays.

THE LIVING ROOM. What's appropriate in a living room is art on the walls, furniture arranged in an inviting way, some collectibles—edited down and artfully arranged to avoid a cluttered look—and things that exemplify the character of your family. What you want to achieve is balance, so the space never looks empty or the reverse—over-packed with personal possessions.

- Consider mounting a bookcase on the wall behind your sofa. It can hold an attractive mix of books and decorative objects that would crowd other living room surfaces.

- Measure the space between windows or between walls and entrances like the illustration on the opposite page, then buy or build bookcases that will hold collectibles as well as books, taking up minimal amounts of floor space in the room.

- Choose bookcase units that combine open shelving (top) with one or more closed cabinets (bottom). Arrange books and collectibles on the open shelves; store coasters, trivets, ashtrays and other small accessories neatly behind closed doors.

A pair of formal étagères fill the wall between tall windows in this suburban living room (left). Each has surfaces for books and objects the homeowners want to showcase. There is also a pair of drawers to hold convenience items that do not go on display.

Glass shelves set into a steel frame (above) create an attractive storage wall. A coffee table with drawers (below) hides most entertaining essentials. An elegant trunk beneath a console (below, right) is clutter-proof. A wall of cabinets (opposite) keeps books partly visible behind mesh door panels.

FORM AND FUNCTION
"In a living room, small chests with drawers rather than tables with open bottoms will give you vast amounts of storage while anchoring the sofa," says New York City–based Hall of Fame interior designer Jamie Drake.

- When displaying books, select those with the best bindings and arrange them by size. Living room bookshelves require a fairly formal, static arrangement, so this is probably not the place to store dictionaries and other reference works that are likely to be removed and returned often.

- Limit the number of accessories or collectibles you put on display. Too many items on a table or clustered on a wall can be claustrophobic. Displaying a few choice elements creates a more focused, less cluttered presentation.

- Shop for a double-duty coffee table. It could be one that has drawers or a shelf underneath, where a few magazines or books can be stacked. (Beneath that shelf or row of drawers you will be able to find room to tuck in extra sofa pillows—rest them right on the floor.)

- Instead of a new coffee table, why not bring in an attractive old trunk that can provide an interesting focus and also hide extra pillows and throws beneath its hinged lid?

Molding-height bookcases are tucked between windows—built-ins made specifically for sections of wall that would otherwise have been dead spaces (above). The coffee table in this farmhouse living room has a relatively deep storage drawer, as does the lamp table beside the sofa.

With the lid on, it's a fabric-covered ottoman on wheels that comes in two convenient sizes (left). With the lid off, each becomes great mobile storage.

- Take advantage of unused corners and the empty walls between or beneath your windows. Adding attractive bookcases would relieve some of the storage crunch and also create another dimension of decorating interest in your living room.

- Embellish your furniture plan with a hassock or ottoman. It can supply not only a place to rest your feet, but also a surface on which to rest a serving tray when you entertain.

- For bonus storage, shop for a hassock with a hinged upholstered top; it's a tidy place to store coasters, playing cards and other small items you might prefer to keep handy.

A fruitwood ladder shelf (above), with five shelves, is flanked by two matching corner units. When positioned this way, these three pieces add up to one strong decorating statement. An upholstered ottoman (left) adds seating to this living room and also doubles as a coffee table.

THE DINING ROOM. To expand a dining room's storage potential, opt for one large cabinet—a hutch, sideboard or buffet. Its top can be an excellent serving station; its drawers and cupboards will hold china, flatware, trays, table linens and perhaps a few of your best serving pieces.

- Consider a sideboard alternative: a beautiful dresser, armoire or any large chest of drawers could be a space-saving substitute.

- If your dining room pieces can't hold all you need to store, think about adding a plate rail to one or more of your walls. It can be a decorative as well as highly functional touch.

- Is there room behind a dining room door to build in or attach a shelving unit to the wall? Even shallow shelves can be a convenient place for glassware, cups and saucers that would otherwise clutter your closed cabinetry.

- Bolt a single drawer unit from a home center to the underside of your dining table, taking care that it is shallow enough not to compromise a diner's knee room. It could become the perfect place to store linen napkins.

An arrangement of family pictures rises above the capacious sideboard in this airy dining room (opposite). A hutch with drawers and cupboards (below) can hold most of a dining room's serving needs. The open shelf and those behind glass are for display.

A long shelf beneath the white crown molding wraps this dining room (left) in storage. A red-and-green-painted ladder placed beside the room's open doorway doubles as a hallway table and display shelving.

DINING ROOM RUDIMENT

"Decluttering this space is not about decorating," states Atlanta-based architectural interior designer Vern Yip, a cable-TV star on the Fine Living Network. *"It's about having a purposeful space plan and selecting furniture that has functional storage. Here, closed cabinets work best."*

- If your dining room is small, moving the table off-center when not in use—against a wall or a bank of windows—will make the space feel less crowded.

- To house an overflow of books or antique treasures, why not add to the dining room architecture by building or placing a bookcase on either side of the doorway? Each unit will absorb some wall space, but being only about 10 inches deep, it will encroach very little on floor space in the room.

- Keep books, stacked plates and vast arrangements of collected treasures off your dining table. It need not stand empty, however. Candlesticks, an ever-changing floral arrangement or a bowl of fruit can provide a needed accent without cluttering the look.

- Liberate a dining room corner and park an elegant storage cart there. You can keep your most attractive coffee maker on it plus tea sets, dessert plates, even a selection of liqueurs. The beauty of such a cart is that it can be rolled to wherever it's needed.

Frosted-glass cabinets extend from the kitchen into the dining area (opposite), uniting both spaces and, with so much available storage, hiding any possible clutter. In a dining room with a window wall that would have been wasted space (above), a homeowner used custom cabinets and open shelving to create an elegant library effect. Another dining room library (left) is at one end of a long living room. The shelves hold books and pictures in many sizes.

2 CASUAL SPACES

"NO MATTER WHAT THE ROOM IS, its purpose should always be clear," says Jamie Drake, ASID, a New York City–based designer. Thus, for him, a family room should look as though a family inhabits it; a breakfast room should be a place where casual meals can be enjoyed; a media room should be a comfortable place to listen to music, watch TV or play DVDs.

What all of these spaces cry out for is order, but the rooms that are used the most are usually taken for granted. According to Shelley Morris, an interior designer in Bedford, New York, people eventually stop seeing such a room objectively: "They become so relaxed about it that a lot of things are left out in the open that they either don't use or don't appreciate anymore. My trick in looking at a room is to spin around— turn my back a moment, then look back. It's like surprising yourself, seeing the room in a fresh way."

Built-ins in this section of a multiuse family room (opposite) store many of the items that family members use often. One dark-blue bin is for toys; the other, for video gear. A large TV hides behind a pair of green doors. In addition there are open shelves for books and collectibles, plus a chair and work surface in a study corner.

THE ALL-PURPOSE FAMILY ROOM

This is a household's typical gathering spot. It could be a den with a giant TV or the vast extension of an open kitchen. Either way, it's an informal kick-back space where family members relax and feel most comfortable. They chat, read, enjoy snacks and entertain close friends. They also add clutter—it's inevitable— which is why decluttering a den or family room usually involves dealing with every member of a household.

DESIGNER SOLUTIONS. Pros agree that keeping clutter under control can be liberating, but it also makes demands. Jerome Currie Hanauer, a New York City designer, tackles the problem head-on: "The first thing to ask yourself is, 'What do you want to keep and what do you want to discard?'" For him, it's not until some degree of paring-down is achieved that any serious decluttering can take place.

- Add storage furniture to your decorating scheme—a coffee table with drawers or a shelf, for example.

- Keep books on shelving; arrange them by subject matter and label the shelves discreetly to avoid confusion.

Elegant built-ins frame a leaded-glass window in this suburban family room (right). The units are individually lit by panels of recessed ceiling lights, and one unit angles around a corner, ending beside a recessed wall area built to house a big-screen TV.

- Try not to fill every inch of every bookshelf. Leave a little open shelf space and add a few collectibles to create some variety.

- Shop for hinge-lidded storage boxes that can be used as extra tables when serving trays are placed on top. Or, upholster the tops for extra seating or just resting your feet.

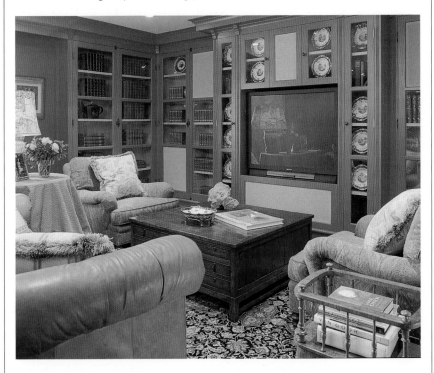

A windowless media room becomes a gracious comfort zone, with cushy seating and red-painted custom woodwork surrounding the TV. Glass-fronted cabinets hold books; open shelving holds collectibles. The centerpiece is an oversize coffee table, with multiple drawers, ensuring that this room is easily kept clutter free.

FURNITURE FINDS. "I see multipurpose furniture—such as an armoire with drawers and open shelves—as part of a trend today," says Michael Amendolara, a Brooklyn, New York, designer. And, Jamie Drake adds, "If it's a small room, I always suggest free-standing pieces. Built-ins will obscure the perimeter, making a small room feel even tinier."

- Instead of closed cabinets, choose storage units with drawers. It's easier to access newspapers and magazines from drawers rather than shelves.

- Look for tables that fold—even sizable dining tables sometimes fold out of cabinets and bookcases—plus storage ottomans and coffee tables that can be raised to dining height.

- Instead of a coffee table, consider a handsome flat-top trunk. The top is useful when serving snacks, and the space beneath the thick lid can hold blankets and throws, or maybe a large-scale toy that you have no room for anywhere else in your home.

CONVENIENCE AND VISIBILITY. "The problem with family room clutter is that things naturally wind up on the floor," says Lou Manfredini, Ace Hardware's Helpful Hardware Man. To rectify this situation, he recommends using mobile shelf units, which can be rolled to the source of clutter, then moved against the wall after everything is neatly put away.

- Keep stored things in sight. The key to good organization is being able to see what you have. Exceptions: your CDs, DVDs and video-tapes, all of which should be tucked away in a cupboard or placed in a closed media box.

- Weed out whatever items you keep in your family room but don't use regularly; pack up, label and store in the attic or basement, or on a utility-closet shelf.

- Don't scatter collectibles. If you're going to display things in the family room, put them in a special place—in a corner or on one or more shelves. Massing things together in a single area will make them look like a real collection rather than islands of clutter.

In a sleekly contemporary family room (below), the TV and music system sit on a blond-wood wall system with a series of double drawers the width of the room. The huge square coffee table has a handy shelf underneath the top surface.

PHOTO FOCUS

"A lot of people tend to clutter their family room with mismatched and poorly framed family photos," Shelley Morris points out. Here is what she suggests instead:

- Pick a theme for your display—it could be different kinds of silver-toned frames, or inlaid wood frames—and choose one style: either traditional or contemporary.

- Arrange all of your framed photos on one or more shelves of a bookcase, or create a kind of collage arrangement on one wall—as a purely decorative element.

- If you do decide to hang your framed photos, select a wall where you and your family can appreciate the images on a daily basis rather than where you usually entertain.

Open shelving—for books and framed family photos—surround the large TV in this sunny family room (above). The corner-fireplace mantel and the coffee table present convenient places to display things. But the bulk of this room's storage needs is fully contained in three two-door furniture-like cabinets that extend the full width of the wall.

There's a cushioned seat at the center of this wall-to-wall built-in (above), which was designed with cubbyholes for shoes and folded clothing. Attractive objects on and above it provide decorating focus. Kitchen cabinets extend into this windowed breakfast room (below), permitting the homeowner, a serious chef, to store her cookbooks behind closed doors. A pair of corner shelf units, mounted high on the wall, supply a stackup of shelves for displaying key collectibles.

TOY STORY. "Store children's toys and games in drawers close to the floor," suggests Lou Manfredini. "You'll make it easier for the kids to pull out what they need and also to put it all back later."

■ Create a defined space for computer games and toy storage, preferably in a cupboard or lidded trunk. When children realize where their favorite toy is kept, they can be taught to remember where to put it when playtime ends.

■ Pull game boards out of boxes, label and store them flat. Place game pieces and accessories in sealable plastic bags; label and drop into a single container. Make a ringed binder for all game directions, arranged alphabetically; store with stacked game boards. Put no-longer-needed boxes in the trash.

GATHERING SPACES

Breakfast rooms and media rooms are informal spaces used mostly by family members, which is why they're so likely to breed clutter: newspapers, serving gear, loose CDs, videotapes and DVDs. As these rooms aren't normally set up for entertaining guests, they are often neglected. And, because they get daily use by nearly every member of a household, their lack of organization is always apparent.

Often a breakfast room is simply an extension of an open or family-size kitchen, which means keeping it neatly organized is linked to kitchen maintenance. Similarly, your media "room" may be one end or one corner of your family room, which is why it's frequently exposed to other activities—reading, chatting, game-playing—that may take place nearby.

A three-sided banquette beside a glass door leading outdoors is large enough to comfortably hold a family of five or six. A niche cut into the wall provides four open shelves for often-used tableware along with bottles of water and a compact music system.

BREAKFAST ROOM. In many households now, family meals are out of the question. People's schedules don't often mesh or overlap. Because of time pressures, lunch or supper might be a quick sandwich or salad at what was intended as the breakfast table. But being in a rush is no reason to be messy. When everything looks organized, keeping it that way is always less challenging.

- Make it easy to set up for an informal meal. Keep everyday tableware handy: dishes in a closed cupboard or on an open baker's rack, napkins stacked in a drawer or napkin holder, flatware laid in a divided drawer or standing tall in a basket.

- Make each family member responsible for his or her place at the table and the area right around it. Decluttering on a limited basis then becomes a simple chore.

- Clear the table after every meal or snack, and put dishes in the sink or dishwasher. Make sure the next person wanting a fast repast has a place to sit and spread out.

- If casual dining is an occasion for reading the newspaper or playing a game, provide shelf space for these items. When family members know where to find what they need before they sit down, they should also know to put them away when they get up.

PLANNED ROTATION
"You don't have to get rid of things you love," urges Carol Weissman, a Leawood, Kansas, interior designer. *"Just don't put them out all at once—rotate your collection, keeping some of it in closed drawers or carefully packed away in storage cartons."*

Red containers set against a bright green wall make this chrome shelving unit —perfect for a TV and stereo gear —a window-wall focus. Its shelves scaled to store DVDs and videotapes, a steel rack (below) is mounted—out of the way—on the back of a door.

MEDIA ROOM. A media room or media corner should include seating arranged with an eye to visual access to a TV screen. The furniture should be inviting and comfortable, of course, but not so cushy that casual TV viewers are likely to nap. The best media-room seating has good support for back, arms and shoulders without providing bedtime-quality comfort.

■ Avoid recliners, or action furniture. They take up too much room and heighten the urge to nod off, no matter how entertaining a telecast or recorded event might be.

■ Furnish with an eye to snacking and dining—TV trays, a '50s concept, remain a good idea because they can be folded and hidden away, decluttering the room when snack time is over.

■ Whether your focus is a large-scale music system or a flat-screen TV, the equipment needs a proper home. Check home centers and mail-order sources for modular units that will hold what you own and ensure that it's organized properly.

■ Keep remote-control units handy—in an open or lidded basket near where they are usually needed. Label each one so its purpose is identified easily.

■ Shop mail-order sources and music retailers for racks and dividers that will help you store CDs, videotapes and DVDs in space-conscious ways—either on shelving or in drawers.

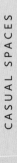

A pair of storage towers flank a two-shelf media stand (opposite, bottom right), all in elegantly detailed pine and stained a dark coffee tone.

This adjustable wall system was assembled specifically to provide easy access to the TV and music system. The shelving offers places to display favorite photos, books and collectibles. The black glass doors beneath the big TV has shelving for CDs and DVDs.

Steel components and walnut-veneer shelving add up to a functional but decorative storage solution (above). Flanking a doorway, they look custom made. An arrangement of freestanding cabinets (opposite) gives this media wall great variety. Collectibles are displayed on open shelves and behind glass doors. A bridge shelf, linked to flanking units, completes the ensemble, which has a broad surface for mounting a big-screen TV.

- Store CDs, videotapes and DVDs near where you'll be using them. Items that are most easily retrieved are the ones most likely to be put back where they belong.

- Arrange your tapes and discs in a prescribed way—in alphabetical order, by category or however you think they'll be most accessible—and make sure everyone else in your household is aware of your system, and thus can help you sustain it.

- No matter how you decide to organize your gear, try to be consistent. That's the best way to ensure you can always find what you're looking for—and also put it back where you've decided it belongs.

- If your music and movie libraries are sizable, catalog each one and keep the listings up to date. This is the best way to avoid any clutter-producing duplications.

- Note that your entertainment catalog need not be a formal record, but it should be a legible one—and kept where it's easily located.

- If you have color slides or old home movies (either the 8- or 16-millimeter variety), be sure to store them away from light, heat and humidity, as their gelatin content tends to deteriorate over time.

- Use drawers or closed cupboards for film storage, or better yet, store anything on film in tightly sealed acid-free cardboard boxes.

- Try to keep cords out of sight. Home electronics tend to involve a tangle of cords that, with some effort, can be clustered and tucked into cord covers that are usually sold at home centers. A cord cover may not make all those many cords disappear, but their presence will be greatly diminished.

MEASURE FOR MEASURE
"Measure the things you want to keep before buying any storage gear," urges John A. Buscarello, ASID, a New York City–based interior designer. *"Whether you're storing books, videotapes, CDs or DVDs, note how much space they require, then allow room for future expansion."*

3 | KITCHEN WORLD

ANYTHING OF IMPORTANCE that occurs in your home today probably takes place in the kitchen. It's not just the heart of the home, it's also the crossroads of family life and household traffic. "A kitchen feeds the spirit of the house," says author-designer Alexandra Stoddard. But since so many people make demands of this spirit-feeding space, disorganization inevitably occurs.

A once outmoded room, the pantry was traditionally a staple of kitchen design but ultimately suffered a decline. Now the tide is turning. Many new homes include pantries with cupboards and shelving, and many cabinetmakers are putting a pull-out pantry near the core of the kitchen. Laundry rooms suffered a similar fate. They fell from favor until it was clear that people wanted a separate space to deal with this essential household chore. Where each of these spaces is concerned, the challenge is keeping them uncluttered.

Countertops and a raised breakfast bar encircle most of this modest-size kitchen (opposite), creating a lavish amount of work and dining space. Wall cabinets—some open, some closed, a few with glass doors— extend all the way up to the wide white crown molding.

TAKING STOCK. Perhaps the best way to declutter your kitchen is to involve the whole family in reestablishing order.

- Pretend you're planning to move or remodel. Empty your kitchen section by section so you can start over, completely fresh.

- Organize essentials; plan to put them where you're likely to need them—ladles and spatulas near the range or cooktop, a knife rack beside a cutting board, canned vegetables on their own shelf in a cabinet or in your pantry.

- Dispose of products you know you will never use—staples that have been on your shelves a long time, for example, or sale items you bought in haste or in bulk. Donate sealed packages and unopened cans to a senior center or homeless shelter, but be sure to toss already-opened boxes and packages.

- Keep track of what you intend to store in each cupboard and drawer, as well as on each shelf. Just note "Silverware," for example, "Every-day China" or any key words that will guide you in assessing and rearranging what you have.

- Isolate what you use regularly from what you need occasionally, and separate canned and packaged goods, cleaning products, cookware and serving pieces.

- If there are packaged goods with a printed shelf life that's been exceeded, have no qualms about tossing the items.

- Check for needless duplications. How many sponges have you tucked away (and probably forgotten you had)?

- With everything out of the way, clean your drawers and shelving thoroughly; consider installing new drawer and shelf liners.

Cooking and serving essentials are kept where needed in this U-shaped kitchen (opposite, top). After removing a base cabinet door (opposite, bottom), the homeowners left room for tall items below their wine cubbies. Open shelves for dishes and hooks for utensils mark this flexible wall system (below).

EXPANDING STORAGE. You may not be able to double the size of your kitchen, but you can certainly increase its storage volume. Before refilling those cupboards, shelves and drawers, think how you can increase their capacity and liberate work surfaces.

- Make every inch count. Installing rows of under-shelf cup hangers will enable you to store at least twice as many cups or mugs as you could if you were to stack or align them on one or more cabinet shelves.

- If you have old cabinets with wide gaps between shelves, add mini-shelf units made of acrylic-coated wire; stack plates and bowls on them neatly by size.

- Hang cutlery on a magnetic knife bar or in a knife storage block mounted under one of your cabinets.

- Install drawer dividers, which can double your drawer capacity and help you keep utensils and tableware sorted for easy access.

Cupboards and drawers on all four sides of this kitchen's rectangular island (opposite) ensure that every essential can be tucked away out of sight. A wall of black tile (top) with yellow, blue and gold insets proves an ideal surface on which to mount steel rods that can hold hanging utensils. Paper towels, a wooden knife rack, spice shelves, a plate rack and a cookbook viewer are all given accessible spaces in this series of wall-hung kitchen organizers (above). White cookware on open shelves, cups and bowls aligned right over the range (left), and a collection of white ironstone platters hung just below the ceiling all add to the cozy feeling that dominates this compact kitchen.

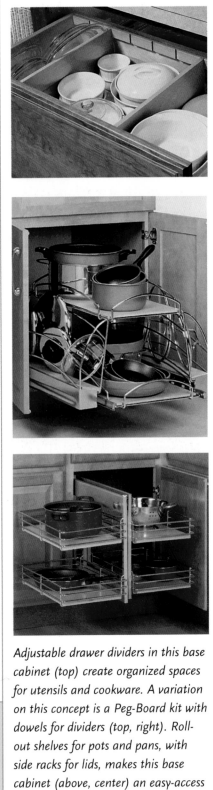

■ Retrofit one or more base cabinets with roll-out shelf units, so you can see and reach items you usually put away.

■ Install carousel units or turntables in pantries and corner base cabinets so neither pots and pans nor packaged goods get hopelessly buried over time.

■ Put walls to work. Peg-Board panels or stainless steel wall systems will let you hang most-used cookware and utensils close to where needed, instead of being stashed in drawers.

■ Hang attractive pots and pans from ceiling hooks or pot racks mounted directly over your cooktop or range. Cookware is handier when you can actually see it and more accessible if you don't have to burrow into cupboards to get it.

■ Unless you are impeded by under-cabinet lighting, consider mounting racks or rails below your wall cabinets; hang a spice rack or a clutch of frequently used utensils there.

Adjustable drawer dividers in this base cabinet (top) create organized spaces for utensils and cookware. A variation on this concept is a Peg-Board kit with dowels for dividers (top, right). Roll-out shelves for pots and pans, with side racks for lids, makes this base cabinet (above, center) an easy-access storage space. Meant for blind corners, this slide-out unit (above) has four adjustable chrome-plated wire shelves. Cookware hangs from a wrought-iron ceiling-mounted pot rack (right).

This base cabinet (left) was designed to provide the ultimate in convenience and accessibility: sturdy drawers—for big pots and small appliances—roll out, and most-used accessories can be stashed on shallow steel racks. A rolling cart (below, left) will hold much of a kitchen's cooking and serving needs. Plus, there's even a rack for oil and condiment bottles.
Every essential is close at hand in the niche created for a cooktop (below). Cookware and large utensils hang from a rod; cutlery and small utensils stand in containers on either side of the appliance.

■ Revive dead space. The unused opening between the top of a wall cabinet and your kitchen ceiling can become a shelf for storing large pots and platters that are only rarely needed.

■ Shop for a rolling cart that can hold cooking or serving essentials, even a microwave, and can be moved around as needed. Carts come in many sizes; some have two or even three shelves plus a butcher-block top that can be handy as a work surface.

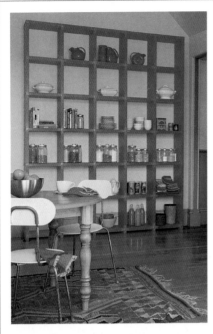

A wall of wood-look cubbyholes (above), assembled from polypropylene panels available as a kit, provides an attractive place to display needed kitchen items. White cabinetry and countertops lend crispness to a country kitchen (right). Its white painted table sparked with stenciled motifs becomes a handcrafted accent. Often-used crockery rests on open shelving above the range, even above the windows. A food processor rises to the occasion on a spring-loaded pop-up shelf (below). When not in use, it's pushed down, out of sight, into a base cabinet.

KEEP ESSENTIALS IN SIGHT. You may find you function better in your kitchen if you can see what you need. Being organized doesn't have to mean hiding everything.

- Add open shelving to the wall space over doors. It's a great place to put covered pots, casseroles and decorative containers.

- If you like to see much of what you store, transfer packaged goods to clear, airtight jars. Labeled properly (including date of purchase) and placed on a shelf or on the counter near your range or cooktop, they can also enliven the look of your kitchen.

- Choose food-storage containers that are square, not round, they'll fit better in corners and stack more readily.

- Hang wire baskets from sturdy ceiling hooks. A dangling trio of such baskets (in graduated sizes) can hold oranges, lemons and ripening pears, bananas or summer fruit.

- ■ Use wire or wicker baskets in base-cabinet shelving to hold potatoes, onions and squash.

- ■ If your kitchen is blessed with unused floor and wall space, a baker's rack can be an effective way to store kitchen essentials that are attractive enough to be displayed.

A butcher-block cutting board, mounted on a painted-wood base (above, left) adds work space. Its oblong shape is no impediment to traffic, and the stacked shelves below capture much kitchen clutter. Slide out shelves with wicker baskets (top) create a handy place to store fresh vegetables. Another variation (above) features elongated baskets placed on narrow shelves, spaces that might otherwise be wasted. Nearly everything in use is on display in a kitchen filled with antiques and found objects (left). The homeowner hangs kitchen essentials on the wall, displays them on open shelves and tucks them on and under a bench.

REORGANIZE LOGICALLY. After accessorizing and increasing your drawer, cupboard and shelf capacity, put back what you removed according to where you need to use it—wax paper and plastic wrap near the microwave, for example, pots and pans near your range or cooktop.

- Store spatulas, ladles, wooden spoons and other long-handled utensils in a large crock, oversize mug or attractive container. Vertical storage can save precious inches.

- Review your cookbooks. Which ones do you turn to often? Which are more entertaining than useful? Which haven't been opened in years? Keep frequently used volumes on a convenient kitchen shelf; place others elsewhere.

- Store surplus supplies, packaged foods and cleaning products in a utility closet or in the basement—anywhere but in precious kitchen space.

- Keep seasonal cooking and serving gear separate. Huge trays, roasting pans and cookie sheets used mainly around the holidays, can be relegated to a high shelf or distant storage—in your attic or basement.

Canted for easy viewing and access, this corner cabinet (above) has niches for a TV and microwave plus a shelf for cookbooks and displayable objects. A roll-up tambour door hides this kitchen's small appliances. Glass shelves behind clear-glass doors (right) make everything stored totally visible. Canisters, standing cup racks and cooking utensils in a tall pottery jar (opposite) present countertop storage in an efficient, highly organized way.

Individual compartments in this pull-out base cabinet unit (above) keep spices and bottles off the counter by standing them upright in a drawer. The awkward leftover space in a base-cabinet system can be put to good use with this pull-out mini-pantry (right). Its chrome-plated steel shelving is spaced appropriately to make room for short spice jars and tall oil bottles.

TO FREEZE HERBS

Dill, parsley, chervil and fennel freeze well. Wash and dry them thoroughly. Discard large stems. Put the herbs in an airtight, rigid plastic container and freeze them. Date the container and use the herbs within a year, using them as you would fresh herbs (no need to defrost). Basil also freezes beautifully, and many people like to make and freeze huge amounts of basil pesto when basil is at its best. At the least, purée the basil with olive oil and a little salt before freezing it.

STORED SEASONINGS

Keep dried herbs and spices off of your countertop. Whether you store them in a wall rack mounted near your range or food-prep zone, or stash them in a drawer, arrange them as your grocer would—alphabetically. It's the best way to keep track of what you have on hand as well as what you'll find you need to restock.

- While organizing your spice rack or drawer, do a thorough inventory. Items you've had for years but never used can be tossed; duplications can be shared with a neighbor.

- Sample a pinch of each spice and herb. One sniff will tell you whether to keep or toss the container. Note that dried spices inevitably lose their fragrance, thus their potency, after a year in storage. Herbs will diminish in flavor after just six months.

- If you find you need additional storage, hang shallow plastic-coated wire shelving on the inside of cabinet doors; it will conveniently hold small condiment bottles as well as spices.

"To declutter a kitchen, I think you're better off making everything open and accessible as opposed to putting it all in drawers or behind closed cabinet doors," says kitchen designer Heather Moe, of South Pacific Kitchen and Construction, Inc., in La Jolla, California. *"What you can see, you know you have and won't have to go hunting for."*

SAFETY & SECURITY

■ Never leave sharp knives loose in a drawer. Store them out of children's reach—if not on a knife bar or in a knife rack, then in a standing block pushed near the back of a counter.

■ To keep a fire extinguisher handy without adding clutter, hang it on a wall or tuck it into a corner of an open shelf. The manufacturer's instructions will tell how close to cooking appliances the extinguisher should be.

■ Keep trivets handy in a drawer or on the counter near your range or cooktop. You always want a safe spot for a hot pot even if your countertop is crafted of high-quality, heat-resistant material.

■ Don't overload electrical outlets. It's better to cluster small appliances in various spots than to gang them all up near one outlet and risk blowing a fuse or breaking a circuit.

■ Always store cleaning supplies out of children's reach; keep such products in their original containers so safety information and instructions are never lost or overlooked.

Stash cooking essentials in these shiny tins (top) that hang from black-lacquered galvanized steel rods. Chef's knives, scissors and sharpening steel each has a home in this cutlery storage block (above), which can stand where needed on a countertop work space. In what's usually dead space under a sink, this shallow drawer (left) is a catchall unit for storing essential kitchen miscellany.

PANTRY REPRISE

A pantry can be a separate space, a functional corner or just a pull-out shelf in the core of your kitchen. The form it takes is less significant than this fact: "The pantry is coming back," says Dianna Holmes, a Markham, Ontario–based kitchen and interior designer. "It disappeared for a while but has returned now, and organization is key."

- If planning a pantry, make sure to include adjustable shelving so reorganizing is possible as your needs change.

- Create pantry shelves where none exist by harnessing spaces between wall studs. A skilled carpenter can cut into a wall and inset shallow units perfect for storing small condiment jars.

This pull-out pantry unit (top) has fixed shelves that can be reached from two sides. An even more capacious variation is this double pantry (above): Each unit has five shelves—enough storage space to hold all of a kitchen's packaged staples. What was once a wide, shallow closet became a pantry (right) when shelves were added and two solid wood sliding doors were replaced by wood-framed glass panels.

Everything is visible and easy to reach in this jam-packed pantry (left), a separate room with its own glass-paneled door. The freestanding storage unit has acrylic-covered wire baskets both shallow and deep, and all of the wall-hung shelving is fully adjustable as storage needs change. No need to bend and dig to retrieve whatever you've stored in this base cabinet (bottom). The shelves pull out readily, and each door is backed with a series of shallow steel racks that hold a vast array of kitchen needs.

- Piggyback a door. If you have a separate pantry, utility closet or laundry room, hang shelves to maximize the back of the door.

- Whatever form your pantry takes, store most-used items near the front of each shelf so they are always within arm's reach. The most efficiently organized pantry not only holds a lot but keeps nearly everything in view.

- Group canned goods, condiments, beverages, packaged foods and other like items so they are all in one place and easy to locate when you need them.

- Find alternative space for any non-food items that find their way to your pantry. Cleaning products and paper towels belong in a utility closet,, shampoos and disposable diapers in bath storage.

- Keep dry pet food in large plastic containers; be sure to label them, and always keep a scoop handy.

ORGANIZING THE FRIDGE

Your refrigerator and freezer are breeding grounds for clutter, not only because of their size but also because of the way they're often utilized. Items that are pulled out frequently—juices, milk, cream, soda—get prime placement, obscuring other items that tend to be lost and, in time, forgotten.

Not long ago, refrigerators required periodic defrosting, which compelled homeowners to clean them and inventory the contents. Today's frostfree appliances generally encourage neglect, so much so that most refrigerators contain items that may no longer be truly edible or needed.

- Empty your refrigerator and clean the interior thoroughly, according to the manufacturer's instructions. (A good time to do this is just before making a major trip to the supermarket.)

- Check for spoiled foods (your nose will tell you), wilted produce (your eyes will tell you) and duplications.

- Check the expiration dates on packaged foods—in your freezer as well as your refrigerator. Be ruthless about disposing of any food that's been stored for more than six months.

- In refilling the refrigerator, group like items together, and place recent purchases behind items that have been around awhile.

- Make sure leftovers are placed in the smallest container possible—not only to save space but also to recognize the fact that less air in containers means less chance of a bacterial invasion.

- Date your leftovers as well as every item you store in your freezer; frequent label review will help you keep track of items still edible.

EGGS

Buy eggs only from refrigerated cases; then get them into your refrigerator as soon as possible after purchase.

Leave the eggs in the cartons, where you should find them packed with the wider end up. Do not shelve them in the refrigerator door where the temperature fluctuates each time that door is opened. Eggs keep well if they are stored properly—at least three weeks beyond the expiration date printed on the carton.

FISH

Freshness makes all the difference in the way fish tastes. Refrigerate fish as soon as you get it home. Use it within one or two days, or freeze it. The colder the storage temperature, the less rapidly the fish will spoil.

If you have a fisherman in the house, it's good to know never to store ungutted fish, which spoils quite rapidly. Non-oily fish such as flounder, sole, red snapper and tilapia freeze best.

Wrap individual fillets in plastic wrap before freezing them spread out on a baking sheet. When fish is frozen hard, pack several fillets in a zip-top bag. This allows you to easily take out just one or two fillets at a time. Freeze fillets for up to six months.

MEAT

Store meat in the coldest part of the refrigerator as soon as you get home from the market. Lamb can be left in its original wrapping. Cuts not prepackaged can be stored in the butcher paper. Keep ground meat no longer than 24 hours.

If you decide to freeze it, wrap or tightly overwrap meat with foil or plastic wrap. Fresh meat can be frozen up to nine months, but ground is best used within four months. When using freezer bags, be sure to squeeze out all of the air before sealing the package.

This laundry room (above) is fitted out with both open and closed cabinets plus a utility sink and a rod on which to hang clothing to drip dry. The same-model appliances stand side by side on a wall containing cabinets, shelves, pull-out baskets and hanging rods (right). Striped wallpaper and a built-in intercom (opposite) lend importance to a laundry room whose wall-mounted cabinets have open shelves as well as closed cupboards. An over-size washer and dryer stand beside a freestanding laundry sink, maximizing the efficiency of a narrow room.

CLEVER COMBO

"Why not set up a room as a pantry that's also a laundry room?" suggests designer Heather Moe. *"You can put all of your foodstuffs on one side, and on the other side you can have the washer/dryer and all of your cleaning products."*

LAUNDRY ROOM SOLUTIONS

"Clutter is just stuff that's not organized," insists Kitty Bartholomew, a design consultant and cable TV personality. Where laundry rooms are concerned, she explains that she prefers to "think vertically rather than horizontally. If you put things on a table, a countertop or a washing machine, you invariably get clutter. But if you store things vertically—on shelves or in cubes stacked on shelves—the look is more organized."

Here's what she did in her own home in Santa Monica, California. On the wall above her appliances she mounted Peg-Board panels, with hooks and flat-back baskets that allowed her to create a storage system for laundry supplies. "The baskets hang against the Peg-Board, and I put my laundry products in them," she explains. "The baskets are at eye level, so even though I don't see all of each container, I do see the tops and know the shapes."

■ If you prefer hiding your laundry storage, why not build a series of under-counter shelves? You can cover them with a curtain on a spring-rod as long as there are two vertical surfaces to support it.

Built-in cabinetry turns a finished basement (above) into a laundry room and home office. Washer and dryer have their own niche, and there is a rod for drip-drying clothes. Adjustable wall-mounted shelving makes the wall behind a home laundry a useful storage facility (right).

- Another way to organize a laundry room is to install a horizontal shelf above your washer and dryer, or a hanging bar. Any way you can get such laundry room staples as detergent, bleach, stain remover and dryer sheets up off the floor and into a spot where you can reach them easily would be a plus.

- If you have front-loading appliances, you can top them with a long, continuous counter. It's the ideal place for folding clean clothes, and it will also prevent socks from falling down between the washer and dryer.

LAUNDRY ROOM ESSENTIALS

- A basket, hamper or rolling cart that can alternately hold soiled and clean items. A two- or three-compartment container would be the best way to keep everything separated appropriately.

- A pole or wooden dowel from which just-ironed or drip-dry clothing can be hung on hangers.

- A flat surface, counter or smooth-top appliance on which clean laundry can be sorted and folded.

- Shelving, cabinets or baskets for laundry supplies.

- A wall rack to hold an iron and ironing board, or an ironing center with an electric connection and a fold-down ironing board.

The mobile laundry station (above, far left) rolls where needed. There is a rod for freshly ironed clothes, and its stain- and moisture-resistant canvas hamper has two compartments, to ease presorting. The rolling triple sorter (above, center left) has a hinged shelf for folding laundry plus three removable, washable canvas hampers. A space-saving over-the-door drying rack (top), which folds up when not in use, has hooks and rods for hanging damp clothes. Rafter-hung shelves create storage (above) where none would otherwise be possible.

4 PERSONAL SPACES

BEDROOMS ARE CONCEIVED AS REFUGES—places where you lounge, dress, undress, sleep. In some homes the master bedroom is part of a suite that is totally separate and private; in other homes it may be more prominent, thus visible to any visitor. Clutter never plays favorites. Even if a bedroom is only seen by those who uses it, disorder can make it less of a retreat and more of a source of chaos.

Guest rooms and kids' rooms present particular challenges. It can be discouraging for a guest to enter a room and find no convenient place to unpack. Equally disturbing is the children's room that is so cluttered that its inhabitants no longer feel comfortable in it. And anyone who does desk work at home knows how important it is to maintain order—so that important papers can be tucked out of sight when no longer being worked on.

This antique trunk (opposite) was a flea-market find that a homeowner refinished before placing at the foot of the bed. Here it becomes a functional as well as attractive accessory. The top of the lid presents another usable surface, and beneath that lid bed linens, a throw and extra pillows can be kept.

Shelving within this multiuse cabinet (above), which is nearly five feet tall, can hold a great many of the items that tend to clutter a bedroom. And when a small mirror is placed behind the drop-leaf, it can be used as a stand-up dressing table. In this red-painted bedroom (right), the night tables have open-work sides plus a shelf deep enough to hold a stack of bedside books and periodicals.

THE MASTER BEDROOM. The beauty of having a bedroom is also having a door. You can shut it and hide the mess—from everyone except, perhaps, yourself. So, the first step in organizing your bedroom is playacting: Pretend that company is coming and you have only a short time to start the cleanup and end the clutter. Keep in mind that this is personal space. Think of it as a kind of retreat, the sort of room you should be happy to come home to. If it's neat and clutter-free, you will always feel welcome there.

- Decide how you want the room to look. Serene? Organized? Homey? Certainly free of clutter and debris.

- Clear off every flat surface: bureau, dressing table, nightstands, bookshelves. Sort the contents and decide not only what to keep but also what to display.

A chest with three deep drawers for sweaters, socks and underwear becomes a versatile storage container with two spacious top drawers—for jewelry, handkerchiefs, folded scarves and almost any other small objects.

- Separate seldom-used and seasonal items from those you tend to reach for every day. Label them, pack them up if you can, and find storage space elsewhere.

- If the room is shared with a spouse or partner, make sure each person has equal breathing space.

- If the room has space for reading or watching TV, does it have a comfortable chair and lamp?

- Is the TV placed so that someone watching it will not disturb someone who may be trying to sleep?

- Can you position the TV so that it is neither too prominent nor the first thing you see when you enter the room?

- Consider having a cabinet in which to store the TV when not in use; you'll find that it makes the room feel considerably neater.

One end of a room was turned into a sleeping alcove (right), with privacy provided by darkening curtains that can be pulled shut. The bed platform was built high enough to allow for a series of storage drawers—some shallow, some deep—underneath. This white-painted two-door cabinet (below) not only keeps that inevitable bedside clutter behind closed doors, it also has a writing shelf that slides out—so all those late-night thoughts, notes and reminders can be recorded.

FURNITURE CHOICES. A bed is obviously the dominant element of any bedroom and also the focal point. As such, it consumes more space than the other pieces, necessitating a careful furniture plan that will keep the room looking and feeling uncrowded. When creating or revising the plan, imagine trying to wend your way sleepily to the bathroom at 3:00 a.m.; you won't want to be bumping into chair legs or tripping over footstools in the dark. The fewer pieces you have, the better. An organized bedroom is spare.

Storage is always an issue, so give careful thought to whatever furniture you decide to put there. It's not enough to buy attractive pieces for a bedroom; it's equally important to consider function as well as form.

- If your dresser is no longer adequate for your needs, why not replace it with an armoire? A taller piece, an armoire can contain a lot of stored items behind closed doors.

- Make sure your nightstands are not just tables but also pieces of furniture with shelving and at least one drawer.

- Put only the book or magazine you are reading on your nightstand; put other books in a bookcase—here or in another room—and confine magazines to a rack near your reading chair.

- Keep tissue boxes and eyeglass cases off the top of your nightstand and in a drawer instead. You might want a decanter and a glass beside the bed, a reading lamp and an alarm clock, but that's all.

- To liberate more space on your nightstands, eliminate the table lamps and mount swing-arm lamps on the wall behind your bed.

Built-in bookcases (left) flank a niche just wide enough for a bed to slide in. For decorating power, transfer prints were painted above the headboard and the built-ins, adding color and pattern as well as unifying the space. An upholstered bench at the foot of the bed adds seating and softness. Shown partly open, the 25-inch-wide bamboo-leaf lidded storage box (below) is shallow enough to fit under a bed but also attractive enough to be kept on display.

- If you really must be surrounded by books, collectibles and other miscellany, consider setting your bed into a custom headboard that includes shelving and perhaps also built-in lighting.

- Organizing the drawers in your bureau or dresser will enable you to store more clothes in less space. Make sure you have drawer dividers, available from closet shops and home centers, so that stacking your garments is easier and more space-efficient.

- To deal with surplus storage, shop for an attractive old trunk to position at the end of the bed. It can hold extra pillows, quilts and even some off-season clothing pulled from your closet.

- In lieu of a trunk, shop local thrift stores for a traditional flip-top piano bench. It won't hold as much as a trunk or chest, but it will provide a surface on which to pile extra blankets.

Blue and white add up to an inviting space (above) that has both serenity and crispness. It has functional storage —in a nightstand with two shelves as well as a drawer and a basket for periodicals. The upholstered seat at the foot of the bed is a convenient place to keep extra blankets.

- Take an all-important first step toward decluttering the room: Make the bed. *Always.* You'll find that makes a big difference.

- Depending on the style of your room, you may want to consider adding a molding strip just above shoulder height. Mount pegs or hooks on it at intervals—to hold shawls and nighties.

- To make your under-bed storage even more convenient, add a set of wheels or casters if there is clearance room. You'll find that they will make those drawer units much more reachable.

- Don't neglect the space beneath your bed. You probably have room there for extra bedclothes, boxes carefully packed with holiday dec-

A dressing table on casters (above) can go where you need it. Beneath its flip-up mirrored top, all your beauty secrets can be kept out of sight. There is a lot on display in this bedroom (left), but most of it is clustered on tables flanking the bed or on a tray placed on the ottoman. The most attractive accessories line a shelf mounted on the wall above the bed.

orations or anything else that is not needed often or is too big to fit neatly in a bureau drawer or on a closet shelf.

■ Recycle the drawers from an old chest you may have relegated to the attic or basement but never got around to discarding. They can become under-bed storage bins. (You can also purchase shallow storage-drawer units from mail-order sources.)

■ Consider the wall beneath a bedroom window to be "found" rather than "lost" space. Tuck a small chest or shelf unit there to hold items that might otherwise be homeless.

DEALING WITH SMALL STUFF. This is the greatest source of clutter—the little things that are perennially exposed, crowding the tops of chests, bureaus and tables, because there seems no logical place to put such things.

■ If you cannot keep small stuff out of sight, contain it—beautifully. A bowl or a basket would be the ideal receptacle for wallets, watches, keys and loose change. Anything else should be kept in a drawer.

■ If drawer space is limited, look for handsome lidded boxes—fabric- or leather-covered, or in an elegantly finished wood. Placed on top of a dresser, they will hold the small items you need most often.

■ Clear that array of little framed family pictures off the tops of bureaus and chests. Find a wall to hang them on—so they can be visible without cluttering your precious surfaces.

HIDE AND SEEK
"In bedrooms, store all but essentials in drawers or behind doors," says Carol Weissman, a Leawood, Kansas, interior designer. "A lot of things that are necessary to live with are not necessary to have sitting out."

SPECIALIZED BEDROOMS

Whether it's a bedroom used by guests or one for your children, it should be a special place that always says "Welcome." The people who visit your home need room to move around in and space to set out what they bring along with them. Similarly, children need room to keep a huge variety of possessions—games, toys, video games, CDs and videotapes, sports gear and clothing—as well as a comfortable place to sleep.

THE GUEST ROOM. That's what it was once called—the "extra" space that is now often a hobby room, sewing room, music room, library or home office. Although it may only rarely house guests, it should be furnished so that if guests do turn up, they will be comfortable and quickly feel at home.

■ Keep a supply of empty hangers in the guest room closet, and keep to a minimum any hanging storage you decide to put there. Clothing stored in zippered bags is less likely to get in the way of overnight visitors.

■ Always reserve some closet space for the possibility of guests—so their shoes have a resting place and their empty luggage can be tucked out of the way. You should not have to rise at dawn and rush to reorganize the guest room to prepare for the arrival of Aunt Mabel on the afternoon train.

■ Keep a minimal amount of furniture in your guest room. A chest with only one or two decorative items on top will be put to good use whenever your houseguests decides to unpack, unless the drawers are already stuffed with storage.

■ Limit the amount of decorating. A clock, a radio, a book or two, plus a comfortable easy chair and a lamp are the only elements, other than the bed, that a guest room requires.

■ Don't allow the room to become spillover space for items that really belong elsewhere in your home.

■ If the room also has a TV set, make sure to have an up-to-date TV listing on hand for your guests' late-night or early-morning viewing. It would also be a good idea to print out how-to-use instructions and attach them to the bottom of the remote.

A nightstand with two wide drawers (above) plus a tray table at the foot of the bed present organized surfaces in this French country bedroom. Two long, low containers (below) provide under-bed storage. One zips shut and slides; the other is open but on casters. Both disappear readily on cue.

Twin beds (above), giant storage bins that slide out of sight, chests, shelves and mini-drawer units—this kids' room has them all, and in a blaze of color. Two nine-bin organizers (right) are placed side by side but could be stacked, if desired. The bins slant down slightly, so what they hold can be reached easily yet won't fall out.

THE CHILDREN'S ROOM. Keeping a child's room organized is an ongoing chore, one that is best managed when you have the active participation of the child or children who use the room. Share the "privilege" of organizing the space, so youngsters will see that they have a stake in decluttering it successfully.

Depending on your children's age, toy storage may be a greater or lesser concern. Before deciding where to store all the toys, it would be wise to review them—to see which ones should be kept and which given away. Toys that are found to be worn beyond repair may simply have to be trashed.

- Group the keepers by category, so that a child can find his or her favorite puzzles, board games, stuffed animals, dolls and video games without having to dig through everything placed in drawers or stacked on shelves.

- Store vertically. A shelf mounted on a wall near ceiling height is the perfect spot for displaying child-crafted items, trophies earned or treasured books. Ceiling-high shelves should have good storage capacity, but the objects placed there should not be anything a child will need to get at often.

Plywood shelves attached to a wooden frame (above) get a whimsical lift with bright purple paint. The desk chair adjusts to any height; the desk, well proportioned for kid use, comes from a kit of ready-to-assemble pieces.

AFTER

BEFORE

Furniture was arranged around the periphery of a teenager's bedroom (above) until Toronto-based interior designer David Overholt entered the scene. He divided the room into two zones. One is for sleeping; the other (left) has become a studio—with chairs, a table and wall-to-wall shelving designed to hold everything from family photos to a music system.

Tucked into the eaves of a two-story house is a built-in kids' closet beside a sleeping nook (above), which has under-bed drawers for extra bedding, sports gear or toys. Metal storage lockers (below) are not just for gym or school use. Brightly painted, they can be equally at home in a child's room or a mudroom. Inside, there is shelf space plus side-wall and overhead hooks. Designer David Overholt used a wall of open shelving to set off the sleeping area (opposite) of the bedroom he created for a client's teenage daughter. The geometric pattern of the bed cover is echoed in the arrangement of square-framed mirrors he hung on the wall immediately behind the bed.

FURNITURE FACTS. Trundle beds and bunks leave more floor space for child's play, but beds that top built-in drawers are equally effective space-savers. Dressers are also important for storing boxed toys and games as well as clothing, but open shelving—either freestanding or built-in—is truly ideal, not only for books, videotapes, DVDs and CDs but also for toys that may not fit neatly into toy boxes or onto overhead closet shelves.

When kept visible, a child's possessions are easier to keep neat. Enclosed spaces in children's rooms invite clutter; having a closed door is likely to conceal disorganized chaos.

- Arrange furniture so there are viable zones—for sleeping, playing and dressing. Chaos and clutter usually occur in kids' rooms when spaces are undefined.

- Make sure your child's room has a table that can be home to a computer or a platform for doing artwork or homework or playing board games. One advantage of a desk is that it has drawers in which paper, pencils, crayons and marking pens can be kept out of sight.

- Where toy boxes are concerned, think small rather than large. A limited number of items can be stored in a modest-size toy box, which can be kept organized easily. A large toy box is likely to become a catchall space—and will always be chaotic, as children try repeatedly to find items that tend to get buried.

- Consider a toy box on wheels, or adding wheels or casters to an existing unit. The box can be rolled into a closet, freeing up floor space when not in use, and pulled out at playtime.

- If saving space is a primary concern, acquire a metal or plastic lidded trash can. Perk it up with paint or colorful decals, and you have a spacious vertical toy-stashing space.

HOME OFFICE

It has been estimated that about 50 million Americans do some kind of work at home, but obviously a great many more of them need office-type space for paying bills, keeping records and answering mail and e-mail. In small homes, an office may be a corner of the living room, family room or den, or a desk crammed into a bedroom. It is the rare home that includes an office as a separate room.

What all these disparate office arrangements have in common is a constant battle against clutter, for where there are files and a desk there are always papers and folders, items to be dealt with, put away or tossed. Staying ahead of the onslaught means being vigilant and superorganized.

"In planning a successful home office, start by making a careful list of requirements," advises Neal Zimmerman, AIA, a Hartford, Connecticut, architect and space planner. "This will not only include workstation space, equipment and power needs, but also social aspects, such as privacy, and whether employees or visitors will enter the mix."

This home office (right) is in one corner of a remodeled kitchen. Overhead cabinets, that match those in the rest of the room, hold most essential supplies. Freestanding units slide under the countertop, an extension of the kitchen work space.

ORGANIZING AID

Architect Neal Zimmerman offers these helpful clues to keeping a home office clutter-free:

- Take time each week to organize what's in your file cabinets; having orderly files will enable you to work more efficiently and will ultimately save you time.

- Remove and inventory your files at least twice a year. Separate them into "active," "passive" or "dead." Only active files should take up space in your home office. Passive files should be stored elsewhere—perhaps packed off to the attic—and dead files should be tossed.

- To maintain an efficient system for storing files, use the same size and type of folders and uniform labels clearly marked with what each file contains.

- For even greater accessibility, color-code your files and note that labels marked with a red star contain tax records; those with a blue star, household bills, for example.

- Keep each individual file folder organized, preferably by date, with the most recent documents up front.

- Do not let papers pile up on your desk. Earmark a place for everything you are working on, and put things away at the end of each project.

Painted storage boxes (top, left) keep this office organized. The wall-hung letter bin (top) has deep pockets for magazines or papers, bills or mail. The fiberboard document boxes (above, center) have label holders and are color-coded for easy identification. An acrylic-covered wire file drawer (above) has color-coded hanging file folders.

A 1920s-style phone and white iron-stone plates on a wrought-iron hanger (above) make this kitchen-corner office a cozy spot. A wall-mounted intercom system links anyone seated at the desk to family members elsewhere in the house. In a more formal space (above, right), a nearly clutter-free desk dominates a corner of a family room that boasts elegantly colorwashed walls.

■ Keep everything except your chair, desk, computer workstation and wastebasket off the floor.

■ If your home office is part of another space, consider adding an attractive folding screen to the room's decor. Pushed open, it can be a simple decorating accent; closed, it will create needed privacy and separation.

■ Furnish the office with pieces that are practical as well as good look-ing—for example, a desk with drawers that can be extended fully without impeding traffic flow in the room.

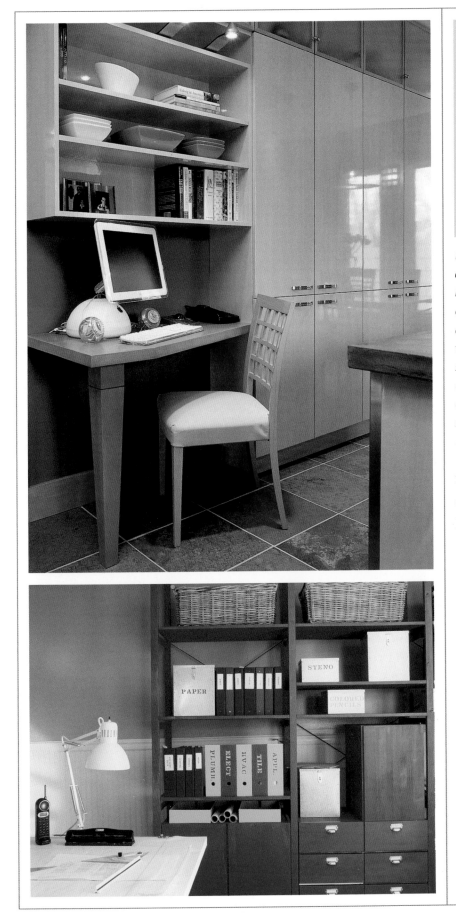

"Make use of pretty baskets—
I have a collection of them on
open shelves in my home
office," says interior designer
Ingrid Leess of New Canaan,
Connecticut. "Using butterfly
clips, I may label one basket
'bills' another 'invoices.' I have
baskets everywhere."

Built-in shelving in the pantry area of
a contemporary kitchen defines a tiny
home office (left). The desktop angles
out beyond standard cabinet depth,
adding more usable work surface for
the homeowner. A drafting table
serves as a desk in this purple-painted
office (below). Binders in contrasting
colors hold important papers; metal
storage containers—some labeled—
keep often-used items close at hand.
The large wicker baskets on the top
shelves, catchall containers for loose
papers and oversize items, add
contrast and touches of warmth.

PERSONAL SPACES

FINANCIAL RECORDS: WHAT TO KEEP. "You need to keep anything that plays a role in your taxes—property taxes as well as federal and local income taxes—for only three years," explains Scott Gutterson, a New York City lawyer and tax attorney. Most other paperwork can usually be disposed of after 30 days.

■ Save paycheck stubs, credit card receipts plus deposit and withdrawal slips only long enough to verify their accuracy. After that, feel free to shred and toss them.

■ Save canceled checks, or check images, for one full year. But if you've written checks for tax-deductible items, retain for three years—in case there's a tax audit where they may be needed.

■ Save bank statements for three years; they may be useful if you decide to apply for a mortgage or wish to refinance a mortgage.

Once the metal strips are screwed into the wall (opposite), it's possible to position brackets that will support a desktop and the storage shelves that are placed above it. Files and supplies find an accessible home in this rolling cart (above) made of white-enameled steel with acrylic-covered wire accessories. The beauty of this storage device is that it goes where needed, then can be rolled out of sight—into a closet or a corner—when work is done. A wooden tabletop fastened to a pair of steel trestles (left) provides a super-size desktop. Behind it is a wall of cabinets plus drawers spacious enough to hold all essential supplies and records. Small items and important papers are kept in containers on wall-mounted open shelving.

5 ORDER IN THE BATH

BATHING, GROOMING, SHAVING, LUXURIATING—a bathroom can be a very busy place, whether it's a master bath, a guest bath or powder room, or a bath used by one or more children. As the locus of so much activity, this room inevitably attracts clutter. Unless you can somehow expand its square footage, you'll need to be inventive to create more storage within the space you have.

"Before you start organizing any bathroom, look around," says Donna Smallin, a nationally recognized space-planning strategist. "What are your biggest challenges? A cluttered sink top? Messy drawers or shelves?" Her solution: Take an inventory of your bathroom, then dispose of duplicate items and anything you decide is no longer usable. Weeding out will not prevent the return of clutter, however, unless you do it earnestly, doggedly and on a regular basis.

Its mirror framed in a Mondrian-like tile pattern (opposite), this vanity has a niche and open shelving for towel storage, plus drawers for all manner of bathroom essentials. When pulled out, the two tall cabinets strongly resemble a kitchen pantry—with shelves that hold a family's prescriptions and cosmetics.

ADDING AMENITIES. Space needs are perennially crucial, no matter how big a bathroom is. Storage capacity is always an issue here, particularly because this is a room that attracts clutter like a magnet. Here are ways to take advantage of every cubic inch.

- If your bath has a vanity cabinet, you can virtually double its interior shelf capacity by attaching vinyl-covered plastic shelf units to the existing fixed shelving—and take optimum advantage of all the available vertical space.

- Put bathroom walls to work by adding single and multiple hooks, not just for robes and clothing but also for towels. Ideally, whatever you need here should be something you can just reach for.

- Fill in wasted space with decorative shelf units designed to fit over the toilet. You can stack washcloths or guest towels there, and perhaps some tall containers as well—for shampoo, conditioner and cotton balls—that might otherwise clutter your countertop.

An over-the-door rack (top), with six giant double hooks, provides hanging space for two tiers of towels. Glass shelves set into two niches (above), plus an open shelf under the sink provide bonus storage in a tiny bath. Dead space behind a bathroom door (right) is turned into floor-to-ceiling storage with this white-painted corner cabinet crafted in the style of an antique country cupboard.

A wall-to-wall shelf (below), mounted a foot and a half below the ceiling, has space to store towels for the whole family. Towel racks and hooks screwed into the tile walls are places where bath linens in current use can be hung and accessed conveniently.

A series of beautifully finished, furniture-like boxes (above), wall-mounted a few inches apart, turn wasted space above the toilet into a storage bonanza in a tiny, contemporary-style bathroom.

FILLING IN THE BLANKS. The space above the toilet is not the only void in the bathroom worth utilizing. "Look higher up," urges Roderick Shade, a New York City interior designer. "I like to put bracket-supported open shelving above a door and extend it all around the bathroom. Place baskets on the open shelves for all those cleaning products, sundries and extra bathroom essentials."

- If you are not keen on open shelving, consider adding a closed cabinet if there is room. When you shop, you'll find that some bath cabinetry has mirrored bifold doors—pulling them open, you get multiple reflections and much more light.

- Look for freestanding cabinets with elegantly trimmed drawers and doors that resemble furniture. You'll find they come in a range of sizes and styles. An extra drawer or shelf unit will give you the option of not having to build storage into a wall.

- Consider cabinets with drawers of different heights. Reserve the deep ones for shampoo, conditioner and other items that can be stored vertically; the shallow ones for hair brushes, hair dryers, shaving gear and other items you usually store flat.

- Whatever type of storage you choose, look for furnishings that can resist moisture, and make sure the manufacturer provides a choice of finishes appropriate for use in the bath.

- Keep your tub deck clear. If you like having soaps, sponges and back-scrubber brushes close at hand, shop for an expandable tub tray that can be adjusted to fit your tub's width and can slide back and forth along the rims of your tub.

A tall cabinet in dead space at the foot of a tub (opposite) has shelves that hold bathing essentials. Another way to keep such items close at hand is to store them in a vintage pie safe (above), adjacent to the tub. Only 13³/₈ inches wide, this stainless steel cosmetics and medicine cooler (below) is double-walled to ensure that its three temperature zones function properly. A stainless steel storage unit that rotates (left) has three toiletry shelves that are hidden when the unit is swung forward, resembling a bland base cabinet. The stainless steel basin rests on a tempered glass countertop.

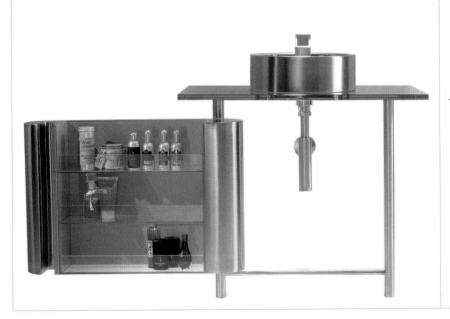

This mirrored medicine cabinet (above) also has a mirror on the inside back wall plus three adjustable shelves. Four inches deep, it can be surface mounted or installed between studs. A pill-bottle organizer (below) fits into a vanity drawer and holds up to 12 containers in a tight grip.

MEDICINE CABINET BLUES. Whether a solo-use storage unit or one that must be shared, a medicine cabinet is a prime clutter-maker. You needn't throw out everything stored there, but you should remove it all periodically and clean the shelves and walls with a liquid household cleaner.

- Evaluate the shelf life and relevance of everything you've stored. Note that even cosmetics, shampoos, sunscreens and over-the-counter medications have defined shelf lives, so look for recommended use parameters printed on package labels.

- When returning items to your medicine cabinet, place new bottles behind any half-used ones to lessen the chance that the refills will be mistakenly used first.

- If yours is a shared medicine cabinet, divide the contents by shelf or half-shelf, so each user knows exactly where to find essential items.

- Even if your bath already has a medicine cabinet, consider mounting another one on an adjacent wall for additional storage.

- When adding a medicine cabinet, look for one with a mirrored front. If you're eager to expand the bathroom's grooming capacity and also to prevent obstructing traffic flow, choose a model with sliding doors instead of a single door that swings open.

CABINET CAVEATS

"I often tell a new patient, 'Put all your medications in a bag and bring them to my office,'" says Dr. Stanley Cortell, director of the Division of Nephrology at St. Luke's-Roosevelt Medical Center in New York City. "I usually end up throwing out at least half of what's in the bag. The prescriptions are either outdated or no longer valid." Here are tips from Dr. Cortell on how to decide what to throw out:

- With prescription drugs and vitamins, note the date of purchase, and get rid of them after a year.

- If you have medication left over at the end of a treatment period, discard it. Don't make the mistake of keeping it to use the next time you think you have the same symptoms.

- Exercise care in disposing of medicines and vitamins. Flush what you can down the toilet; put the rest in a bag, tie it up carefully and put it in a lidded trash can out of the reach of children and pets.

COUNTER INTELLIGENCE. In bathrooms blessed with a vanity, clutter may be strikingly evident, because the counter is so often crammed with items that really do deserve a home. The most useful counter is one that's kept clear and open.

■ If you must keep essentials on your counter, cluster them in an attractive container, such as a basket.

Two drawers were eliminated from a vanity (above), and the third was replaced with a trio of towel bars. The handled drawer front pulls out when the towels are needed. A full-width bottom drawer (left), in addition to standard drawers and cupboard-style shelving, makes this vanity special. With great depth as well as width, the drawer is the perfect place to store surplus items and supplies. A variety of accessories hang from two chrome-plated brass utility bars (below), putting most-used bath needs within easy arm's reach.

■ Organize the cupboards and drawers below your countertop so that every bath essential has its own special space.

■ In a bath used by more than one family member, assign drawers to each person and urge that the contents be kept neat.

■ Utilize drawer dividers, such as those designed for kitchens. They provide a good way to separate items into categories—hair care, nail care, foot care, etc.—and also to make sure that needed items can be accessed easily.

■ Store vertically. Your favorite housewares store or home center will have tiered storage units to place on the counter. These can hold soaps, sponges, washcloths, brushes and other small items that are perennial counter-clutterers.

■ If you have room, suspend a tiered wire basket from a ceiling hook or wall bracket. Such a basket can hold items—sponges, mitts or back-scrubber brushes—that often get buried deep inside under-counter cupboards.

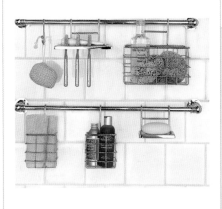

- Find a special place for your electric hair dryer—near a wall outlet, of course, but not so close to the sink or tub that it can ever fall in. Hung from a wall-mounted hook, the dryer will always be handy without cluttering the counter.

This acrylic hair-care organizer (above) can stand on a shelf or hang on a wall. Vintage tableware was the model for these faceted-crystal storage pieces (below). Frosted glass inset into a wood frame (right) turns a tall wall cabinet into generous bath storage.

COUNTERTOP CONSISTENCY

"Look for inexpensive clear-glass containers, either with or without tops," suggests Joan DesCombes, CKD, of Architectural Artworks Inc. in Winter Park, Florida. "Use one for cotton balls or swabs, another for bath salts, another for makeup brushes or emery boards. Separating these essentials makes them easy to access, and storing them in containers of the same size and style is an attractive way to contain items you use often and want to keep visible."

- Store bathroom gear near where you like to use it. If you have to poke into the back of a drawer or burrow deep into a cupboard for items you need regularly, your storage plan is faulty.

- Reserve cupboard space for cleaning products and also for bath supplies: extra boxes of cotton balls and tissue, spare rolls of toilet tissue and other related products that may be important for you to keep handy but probably not to display.

- To maximize under-counter cupboard space, obtain a freestanding lazy Susan from your hardware store; it will ensure that what you store down under is rarely unreachable.

- Harness the back of your cupboard doors. Space-saver shelving in the style of spice racks can hold sponges, cleanser or a selection of bottled toiletries.

- If your bath has a pedestal sink instead of a vanity, consider putting a small, shallow chest, cupboard or shelf unit directly under it—preferably one with a toekick so someone standing at the sink doesn't stub a toe.

- Whether your wastebasket is tucked in a cupboard or left in the open, you can save time and effort by keeping folded-up plastic garbage bags directly under the basket liner in current use. When the basket is full and the old liner is removed, a fresh liner is there for you, ready to put in place.

- Whatever storage aids work best for you, try to eliminate confusion by keeping grooming aids and cleaning products separate.

- Augment towel storage with hooks; they take less space than rods.

BASKET CASES

"I keep pretty baskets on open shelves and on my bathroom counter," says designer Ingrid Leess. "Some hold extra soaps; others, jewelry that I wear all the time. I know from the style of the baskets exactly what they contain, so I'm never in doubt about what to reach for."

Ideal for bath storage is this handy basket (above) made of sea grass woven around a wood frame. An empty window frame with rough-plastered edges replaced cabinet doors in this vanity (left), and shirred fabric adds color and softness. A leaning teak ladder (below) adds vertical storage for towels, accessories and magazines.

SHOWER STALWARTS. Some showers have built-in niches with more than one level so that shampoos and conditioners as well as bar soaps can be stored neatly. But shower stalls lacking such amenities can still be accommodated.

■ Shop for a plastic or metal wire unit designed to fit over the neck of your shower. Depending on its size, the unit will hold bars of soap, a nail brush, bottles of shampoo and conditioner, and very often a washcloth as well.

■ Install floor-to-ceiling corner shelving inside the shower stall to hold soap, shampoo and conditioner. The shelving can be the kind that's suspended from spring-loaded supports, hooked directly on glass shower walls or screw-mounted to tile-covered walls for secure permanence.

A storage tree (above)—wire baskets on a tall tension rod—holds a host of bathing essentials. Depending on household needs, this item can be installed in a shower or one corner of the room. In a bath with a pedestal sink, rather than a vanity (right), an interior designer fitted out a narrow niche beside it with glass shelving.

Built-ins in a sleekly designed contemporary bath (above) include drawers, a bench, a niche for towels and a four-shelf storage cabinet with frosted-glass door insets.

TOWEL ACCESS. If you have the wall space, you can add towel rods or hooks to hang towels near the tub or shower and certainly near the sink. Plus, you should also make room for fresh towels as well as a hamper to contain those waiting to be laundered.

- Unless you find room in your linen closet, plan to store clean towels on open shelving in your bathroom.

- Fold and stack bath towels and washcloths, or roll them up tightly and stow them on shelves near your tub or shower.

- If there's no room for a hamper, hang a mesh laundry bag from a hook mounted on the back of the bathroom door. The bag will hold soiled towels without taking up a lot of space.

Bath storage is visible through glass panels in a vintage-look cabinet (top) with sliding doors. This go-anywhere étagère (above), with four shelves and a drawer, works well in a bathroom. A two-level towel bar and a shallow shelf beneath the counter (right) make this tiny bath great for guests. A storage bench with cushioned seat (opposite) is a dual-purpose bath accessory.

Shirred fabric on a spring rod (top) hides under-sink bath storage and also matches the tone of tongue-and-groove wainscoting. Tall storage bins pull out beneath the counter of a vanity (above) topped by a vessel-style stainless steel sink. Its overall whiteness (right) creates a feeling of spaciousness in a bathroom whose gauzy window treatment adds to an ethereal look. A tall étagère and a modest-size vanity hold all of this bath's needs. A rarely seen amenity (above, right), this tilt-down drawer front hides a tiny storage space for often-used bath essentials.

BIG IDEAS FOR LESSER BATHS

The master bath may be the most challenging one in your home because of its size and the fact that more than one person regularly uses it. But guest baths, powder rooms and children's baths have specific requirements—and reasons to be kept clutter-free.

GREAT FOR GUESTS. A guest bath, like a powder room, should be a serene and inviting space, not one so crammed with overflow items from other bathrooms that a visitor to your home would find it difficult to use. An uncluttered bath is one sure way to make any guest feel welcome. Be sure that:

■ there are towel bars, towel rings or wall-mounted hooks to hold a supply of fresh hand towels, washcloths and bath towels;

■ there is a generous, easy-to-find supply of toilet tissue not only on the exposed roller but also in reserve;

■ there is countertop or shelf space so a guest has room to unpack toiletries, cosmetics or medications;

■ there is light adequate enough for shaving and grooming. If you have counter space, add a table lamp; if not, a floor lamp. A guest bath need not be furnished in any predetermined style or manner.

TOYLAND. That is what many children's bathrooms become, and although these toys may be important at bath time and other moments in the day, they should still have a home.

■ If there is room near the tub for a small, freestanding chest or shelf unit, make sure all toys are put there after use.

■ Depending on the size of the bath, you might want to consider bringing in a cabinet on wheels or casters. Either would be a flexible, practical choice, as it can be placed wherever there's room and rolled beside the tub as needed.

■ If space is tight, install a sturdy hook near the tub; hang a small basket or mesh bag from it so that bath toys can stay in plain sight yet out of harm's way. If kept in the open air, bath toys will dry quickly when bath time ends.

■ Keep a small step stool handy so that young children can always reach what they need.

■ Keep medications and any potentially toxic products—bleach and ammonia, for example—out of children's bathrooms.

Under the cushioned seat (below) in this bath are niches for two wicker laundry baskets that slide out on a drawer-style base. Nonslip rubber feet make this whimsical bin (bottom) an ideal receptacle for bath toys. The holes add interest and also provide ventilation for wet toys.

6 CLOSET KINGDOMS

CLOSETS CAN TAKE MANY FORMS. There are walk-in or double-size closets designed for spouses, utility closets for mops and brooms plus all of a household's cleaning gear. There are hall closets that, depending on location, are either packed with sports gear or set up for guests. There are also closets exclusively for linens and towels, and, of course, closets just for kids' stuff.

Mom and pop closets are key; they tend to be big and also set the tone for closet content and upkeep throughout a home. In addition, what doesn't fit in master bedroom closets tends to spill over into the other ones, thus upsetting a delicate balance. Paring down is an obvious solution. How? Interior designer Christopher Lowell, the Emmy Award–winning host of numerous Discovery Home Network TV shows, has a suggestion: Examine every garment in your closet and ask yourself, "Does this truly reflect who I am today?"

A totally fitted closet (opposite), with rods, adjustable shelves and a three-drawer chest—all wall mounted—is custom rigged to meet the wardrobe needs of the couple who shares it.

Shelving plus rails shown in a satin-nickel finish (top) are part of an easily installed wall system that offers great flexibility. More complex but no less flexible is a system with premeasured clothing rods, acrylic-covered slide-out baskets and pants racks that also slide out (above), for easy accessibility. The forward edges of both shelving and drawers have a subtle walnut finish.

HIS AND HERS

Some people arrange their clothes by color, others by function. It doesn't matter how you organize, only that you do. "We wear only 20 percent of our clothing 80 percent of the time," explains Christy Best, a California-based professional organizer. "We tend to wear our favorites. We don't go into the closet and pull out the stuff that's in the back. We wear what fits us now." Whether yours is a wall closet or a walk-in, and whether it's shared space or all your very own, you will probably find that it can be reconfigured to suit your needs better.

TAKING STOCK. Before buying a single storage accessory, however, take time to remove all of the closet's contents. "Don't just empty your closet and put everything in a big lump," urges Linda Kooper-smith, the self-proclaimed Beverly Hills Organizer. "Sort as you go. I measure the clothes in my closet: For example, how many vertical inches of blouses do I have? Men usually need 40 to 42 inches of length for shirts hanging on a rod; women, usually 34 to 36 inches for blouses. You can store men's pants in a double-hung arrangement because they don't need 42 inches. In that case you can hang shirts on the lower pole of the double hang and pants on the rod above it."

Here are other ideas to consider:

- After emptying your closet, arrange its contents in separate piles: his, hers, hats, suits, jackets, dresses, blouses, shoes—in other words, every applicable category.

- Examine each item. If it is something you haven't worn in the last two years, consider giving it away. (Always be sure to check the pockets first!)

- Weed out seasonal gear, luggage and anything else you can store elsewhere—in the attic, the basement or a back-hall closet.

- Clean the closet thoroughly, including corners where dust usually accumulates. Note that this may be a good time to refresh interior walls and shelving with a new coat of paint.

- Make sure every piece of clothing you put back in the closet is something that still fits, is in wearable condition and—most impor-tant—is an item that's likely to be worn. Damaged clothing can be turned into rags; wearable surplus can go to the Salvation Army, Goodwill Industries or a local charity.

AFTER

BEFORE

The same closet, when organized well, can have breathing space yet hold everything it once did, but in a more visible and accessible manner (above and left). A walk-in closet that's also a dressing room (below) is neatly divided—his on one side, hers on the other. What doesn't hang is folded into drawers in a neutral zone.

Battery-operated, this electronic tie rack (top) holds 54 neckties, has a built-in light—so the right choices can be made—and hangs from any closet rod. In another hanging storage solution (above), sturdy canvas drawers and open shelves, in either a four- or six-unit package, are leather-trimmed.

- If your closet has a solid door that swings open, use it for over-the-door storage accessories. You can also attach dowels or budget towel racks to the door to hold scarves, belts and neckties.

- Keep fine jewelry in a nice box in one of your dresser drawers, but hang long necklaces and other costume jewelry from cup hooks that can be mounted on the wall just inside your closet door or on the back of the door itself.

- Keep shoes off the floor. A modestly priced rack will help you organize them for easy access. Unracked shoes are most likely to scatter, making it difficult to find suitable pairs when seeking them.

- If you prefer shelving shoes in their original boxes, label the exposed end of each box or attach a photo for quick identification. An alternative would be to splurge on transparent plastic shoe bins, which will keep your shoes dry, dust free and visible.

- Zip sweaters into transparent plastic pouches. Or, stack them on open shelves, maintaining order by using vinyl- or epoxy-coated vertical steel dividers to prevent their spilling over each other.

- Isolate convenient wall or door space so you can install stick-on or screw-in hooks for your bathrobe or dressing gown.

- Store handbags where you can see them: arranged on the shelf above your clothes rod or hanging from stick-on hooks on a closet wall. Always organize by color, so that black, brown, beige or navy blue styles are handy when you need them.

- Carefully pack serviceable but seldom-worn clothing in a cardboard box. You can relegate it to the top shelf, way in the back, as long as you put a label on it, listing its contents.

- Set aside a spot at one end of a clothes rod for that ready supply of empty hangers. If allowed to hang among your clothes, they take up space needlessly and also tend to get knocked to the floor, where they immediately create clutter.

Having a lot of space should never justify squandering it. In fact, the more closet space you have, the greater the challenge is to use all of it well. Here are two equally efficient closet systems. Each is designed to fit a specific space as well as particular customer needs. In each, every stored item is visible—from luggage that is stashed on upper shelves to shoes that hang on vertical wall racks.

SPACE SAVERS. In addition to hooks, over-the-door storage and transparent shoe and sweater holders, try these closet storage aids, which you can find at most housewares stores (and be sure to measure your closet first, so whatever you buy will fit the space where you plan to put it):

- Canvas or plastic storage units suspended from hanger-style hooks on your closet rod can hold folded blouses, shirts or sweaters.

- Wire baskets on racks or shelves are great for folded garments you always want to be able to see.

- Hanger units designed to hold skirts and jackets, pants and jackets or multiple pairs of pants use vertical instead of horizontal space.

- Clear, zippered plastic bags help keep folded out-of-season clothing neatly stacked but easy to spot.

- Hat racks can be mounted side by side or in a vertical arrangement on one wall or on the back of the door. Where you hang your hats depends on the space you have, how high you can reach and how you like to access your headgear.

Make a show of hat storage (top) in this stack-up of French hatboxes. A rattan basket (above, center) is a good place for sweaters. A system of drawers with glass fronts (above) heightens closet accessibility. A wall-mounted system turns the corner, making a small closet live large (right).

Individual components, all in a wood-look laminate (left), can be arranged according to individual needs. There are closed cupboards and drawers, open shelving, rods for hanging blouses and skirts, storage bins and baskets for small items, plus cubbyholes for shoes. To make an existing closet system even more efficient, a 20-pocket canvas shoe holder can be hung on one side of a closet door (above).

DOS AND DON'TS

- Do organize your closet so that belts, neckties, scarves, handbags, shoes and sweaters are within easy reach.

- Don't mix sports gear and luggage in with wardrobe storage. Limit your closet's contents to clothing.

- Do ease the closet crunch by expanding your dresser space: Tuck a small chest or trunk under a window or place it at the foot of your bed; either container would be perfect for storing such items as scarves, shawls, T-shirts and gloves.

- Don't keep anything essential on the floor of your closet or at the back of a shelf. If you do, you might as well give it away, because you will probably never see it and forget it's even there.

WISE WORDS

"The key to solving the organization problem is to scale down your belongings to fit your space," says Christy Best, a professional organizer.

ORGANIZING INSIGHTS. The best way to manage clutter is to reduce it. Pare down the contents of your closet by finding other places to stow some of your stuff—in the attic, if you have one, on a shelf in your guest room or under a bed. Here is how to store clothing you want to keep but only rarely wear:

- First, launder or dry-clean what you plan to pack away (sweat and food stains can attract moths). Plus, your clothing will be clean and ready to wear when it's time to retrieve it from storage.

- Whether you store shirts, jackets, blouses or sweaters, fold each item neatly and then tuck tissue paper into shoulder and collar areas to hold the shape.

- When storing folded suits or jackets, use plastic covers from your dry-cleaner instead of tissue paper to soften the creases.

- In lieu of wall hooks for storing handbags and totes, acquire a cubbyhole unit from a home center or unpainted-furniture retailer. Mounted on a wall or placed on a shelf, it will provide easy access to items like these that you reach for regularly.

- To prevent scuffing your favorite handbags, line shelves or cubbies with felt or other soft fabric. Don't seal any handbag in a plastic container; leather needs to breathe.

- Use a wall-hung shoe bag for storing scarves, a similarly mounted necktie rack for keeping belts in order. Each saves space and also keeps stored items visible.

- Put mothballs or cedar chips into every storage container you use. Both discourage moth infestation.

- Keep seasonal items in zippered bags, plastic containers or sheets of plastic taped tightly to ensure a good seal.

- If closet space is limited and your storage needs have reached the bursting point, consider investing in a complete closet organizing system from a nationally recognized supplier.

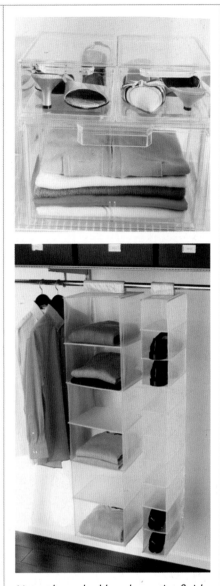

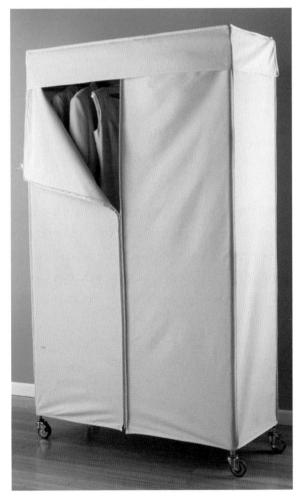

Natural wood adds a decorative finish to this custom closet (opposite), with windowed storage containers for fast identification. Create a closet where one doesn't exist, with a zippered, canvas-covered garment rack on wheels (left). It seals out dust but has some porosity, allowing clothes to breathe. Consider adding this clear-plastic drawer system (top) to make a shelf more efficient. The stackable units can be added to as needed. Another variation on the hang-storage concept is a translucent-plastic shoe and sweater duo (above).

Here is a closet system designed as a gift-wrap station (top), with rods that hold wrapping paper and mini-drawers and cubbies that contain tools and trimmings. A closet just for kids (above) has rods, drawers and shelving that can be adjusted as the youngsters grow. There's also room to keep deep toy bins with handles so they can be pulled wherever needed.

OTHER CLOSET CHALLENGES

Clothes are not the only items that need to be stored in closets. You should also isolate specific spaces in which to put mops, brooms, brushes and all manner of cleaning gear. Because your hall or guest closet should be left mostly empty, so visitors have places to hang their things, you may need a special, separate closet for bowling shoes and ice skates, soccer balls and snowboards (if you don't have a garage).

Even the youngsters in your household should be encouraged to put crash helmets and shoes with cleats somewhere other than in their bedroom closet. Note that skis and other long, narrow items might find an easily accessed home under beds.

CHILDREN'S CLOSETS are a particular challenge. You can probably declutter and tidy yours in half a morning, but that's not the point. If *you* do the organizing, your kids will have no stake in the arrangement and will probably restore the messiness in a wholly frustrating effort to locate the things they want to wear or play with. It's better to set aside quality time so you and the kids can do the decluttering together.

- Empty and clean the closet; inventory its contents, noting and counting everything you find there.

- Separate reusable toys and clothing. Decide what is in a condition good enough to be passed along to friends, relatives or other family members and also what should be donated or dumped.

- Don't put anything back without positive assurance that it will be worn or used.

- Make a kids' closet handy by making sure frequently worn clothing can be pulled out easily. If there is room for double rods, hang school and play clothes on the low rod, seasonal or dressy clothes on the higher one.

- Mount a shoe bag on the inside of a swing-open closet door. That is the easiest way to encourage kids to put footwear away rather than simply drop it on the floor, where it may be lost forever—or until you organize the next closet cleanup.

- Restrict the closet floor to large-scale toys or rolling toy bins that can be pulled out when needed and then rolled back.

A closet created to help a teenager stay organized (above) keeps everything visible as well as uncluttered. Plastic hangers make a color statement but are also useful for identifying seasonal garments or items reached for often. Rods and shelves on two levels make the most of existing spaces without making anything hard to get.

Everything is airy and open in this well-planned linen closet system (right), and every inch of vertical space is made usable. Adjustable shelves hold towels in manageable stacks, and the pull-out drawer units are acrylic-covered steel, so their contents are always in sight. Even extra blankets can be tucked away here but still stay visible in clear-plastic containers.

LINEN CLOSET LORE. After emptying it completely and setting aside items to toss, turn into rags or give away, take time to dust and possibly also paint your linen closet. Line its shelves with acid-free paper that will not bring harm to any items stored there long-term. Before putting anything back, pluck out what could be stored elsewhere. A linen closet should be a haven exclusively for sheets and pillowcases, towels and washcloths, and often table linens, too, but never bowling balls, computer games or books.

- Sort folded towels by size and color. Keep washcloths, guest and hand towels separate from bath towels, and place each stack on a shelf hung at a convenient height for everyone in your household.

- Separate bed linens into stacks earmarked for each bed: fitted bottom sheets, unfitted top sheets, pillowcases, pillow shams. If it is possible, label the shelf under each stack so everyone knows which linens are available for which bed.

- Store extra pillows, quilts, duvets, comforters, blankets and other bulky bedclothes in transparent zippered bags. Place in an out-of-the-way place, either on top or bottom closet shelves.

THE BROOM CLOSET REVISITED. Today, it is called a utility closet, and it usually holds more than brooms. This would certainly be the place to keep a surplus supply of light bulbs, toilet tissue, bar soap and detergent. But it is mainly a place for wet mops, dry mops, buckets and the vacuum cleaner. In some cases, it also holds gear that doesn't belong there but found its way in simply because there seemed no other place to put it.

That's why your first step in organizing the space would be to weed out the ski poles and baseball bats, which could be stored in the attic, the garage or the basement, and include only those items that relate to the general upkeep and repair of your home.

■ Store brooms and mops on clamps attached to the wall. Be sure to mount them far enough apart so that you only get what you need when you reach for it.

■ If your home lacks a laundry room, reserve a spot on a shelf for the iron, and consider suspending your ironing board from hooks mounted on the back of the door. You won't want to drag that item out of the closet every time you need to reach a mop or a broom.

"DON'T SWEAT THE SMALL STUFF," a long-popular maxim, is particularly apt where the utility closet is concerned, as this is the traditional haven for a seemingly endless list of items that often get categorized as junk. It's really miscellany, of course, but all of it may be essential to the successful running of a home.

■ Why not set up a junk box, or perhaps more than one? A shoebox would be good; a similarly sized see-through plastic or acrylic container would be better.

■ Pack the junk box with spare fuses, light-switch plates, wall plugs, rolled-up extension cords and a selection of batteries—Ds and double-As are the most common. Label the box or container in detail, and make sure everyone in the family knows where it is and what it holds.

■ Be prepared for emergencies. A toilet plunger is a must, but you should also keep a small tool kit handy. Stock it with a hammer, large and small screwdrivers, pliers or wire cutters and a basic assortment of nails, nuts and bolts.

Hooks that hold things in a tight grip—brooms, mops and anything else that hangs—make this stainless steel, wall-mounted unit (top) a storage must. It's 27 inches wide, with a shelf that's 4 inches deep. Out-of-the-way, over-the-door storage of an iron as well as an ironing board (above) liberates space in the tiniest utility closet.

7 UP AND DOWN BONUSES

ATTICS AND BASEMENTS—NOT EVERY HOME HAS either, and comparatively few homes have both. But anyone fortunate enough to have such bonus spaces probably takes them for granted, using each of them as a virtual dumping ground for all manner of materials and miscellany for which no room exists elsewhere.

A basement is inevitably the final resting place for leftover gear or treasured junk—stuff that just won't go away. Whether it's a collection of no-longer-needed baby toys or Aunt Margaret's armchair that's been awaiting reupholstery since before the millennium, whatever gets dragged to the basement is seldom ever seen or used again. The same is usually true of the attic, a space that may be talked about by everyone in a household but rarely visited. Why? Because no one can recall what's stored in either space and would be hard pressed to find it even if they did.

A serene corner of this finished attic (opposite) is furnished as a simple getaway space. Set next to a window, with double-layer curtains for good insulation, this is an island of calm in what is usually a virtual sea of clutter.

One end of this attic sitting room (above) is walled-off closet space with double doors that make whatever is kept here visible only when needed. The closet itself is neatly organized with drawers, a rod and shelving—all wall mounted so that the attic holds no secrets.

CLUTTER UP TOP. Homes with attics are usually top-heavy with storage overflow. "I never go up there," one homeowner confesses. "I just can't face it." But facing it, and making it work, really makes life in the rest of the household that much better. For when weeded out and organized well, so that everyone in the family knows what's stored there, an attic can be the perfect repository for those items your family no longer uses regularly but can't live without.

OVERHEAD CLEARANCE

- After emptying the attic and cleaning out the entire space (which may not have been done since before you moved in), separate the items that must be kept from those that should be given away or set out with the trash.

- Before putting anything back, and particularly before adding to the volume of material you decide to store, determine how much weight your attic can support. If in doubt, seek out a qualified home inspector in your local yellow pages.

- If you have an unfinished attic, with no actual floor, you can improvise one by using 1-inch-thick sheets of 4-by-8-foot particleboard or plywood. Whether loosely laid or nailed to joists, these sheets will create a surface suitable for walking and for storing.

- If your attic lacks insulation—under the roof and between ceiling joists directly over the rooms below—installing it can give your possessions longer life.

- Whether you use paper- or foil-backed fiberglass batting, rigid-board or loose-fill insulation, be sure to cover it completely with sheets of foil or plastic after putting it in place.

- To improve air circulation, consider installing gable-end louvered vents at opposite ends of the attic. Good air flow can be an effective way to take the edge off of extreme heat and cold, either of which could be damaging to many of the items you've stored there.

- To preserve anything that might suffer damage from excessive heat, whether your attic has vents or not, think about installing a motorized exhaust fan that's set to switch on when the temperature reaches a particular level (usually 90° or 95° F). Bonus: A cooled attic will help cool the rest of your home in warmer months.

- Upgrade the lighting. If your attic is lit by one lonely incandescent bulb, you probably can't see what you store there.

- Consider installing one or more sets of shop lights, the kind of illumination most craftspeople prefer. These fixtures supply plenty of light and also make use of energy-saving fluorescent bulbs.

- Keep a flashlight and fresh batteries handy. Even with good overhead lighting, you'll need help to see into corners, crates and heavily stacked shelving whenever you have to retrieve any attic content.

- Don't neglect corners; piling everything in the middle of your attic simply wastes space.

- Build gable-end shelving—wide near the bottom, narrower as it rises toward the roof. Note that any containers you put on shelves will always be easier to access than those you stack on top of each other.

- To make the most of every attic inch, buy or build bookcases or shelving to place along the knee wall—it's the wall that often extends below a sloping roof.

- To take full advantage of roof slope, improvise a closet for out-of-season garments. Mount sturdy poles or rods between roof rafters, and be sure to store clothing in zippered bags.

Sixteen drawers in a break-resistant polypropylene unit (top) create compact storage for hardware or craft products. Up to 40 pounds of overhead storage (above), in an attic or garage, pulls down handily when access is wanted. Labeling is not needed for blankets stored in these plastic covers (below). Zippered shut, they keep moths and dampness out.

TO HAVE AND TO KEEP. Loose items waste space and are also hard to safeguard and keep track of. It is more sensible, over time, to store items in wood, steel, plastic or even heavy-duty cardboard containers. Keep in mind that whether you buy, build or salvage shelving, cabinets or containers, your investment will pay off in longer life for the things you store

- Consider using lidded clear-plastic or acrylic containers. You will find them ideal for attic storage because they are lightweight, their lids close tightly and, perhaps most important, their contents will always be visible.

- To protect delicate items that can be damaged when shifted around or affected by heat, cold or even modest temperature fluctuations, wrap everything you store in bubble wrap or old newspapers.

- For basic moth-, dust- and rustproof protection, tightly seal the containers you choose with duct tape, masking tape or heavy-duty transparent tape.

- Store photos and all important documents in fireproof metal file cabinets, which offer optimum protection. You'll also find that they hold more and are easier to access than shopping bags or boxes stuffed with papers or files. (Keep in mind that bargain-priced file cabinets can usually be purchased at thrift shops, tag sales or second-hand office-furniture outlets.)

A roll-down canvas cover hides and seals off whatever you decide to keep in this three-shelf attic storage unit (right). The frame is wood, the shelves are wooden slats, but the unit itself is covered in heavy-duty canvas.

THE ACCESSIBILITY ISSUE. Make copies of each up-to-date inventory you do—one to post just inside the attic door, another for your own files. This way, you won't have to climb up to the attic to check out what's there, and when you do make the trek, you'll know for certain that you'll find what you're looking for.

To make sure that you can always locate whatever you store in the attic, group like things together: heirlooms in one section, valuable papers in fireproof containers in another. If your attic is traditionally a repository for spare quilts and winter blankets, holiday decorations or cold-weather clothing and gear, put them where you can see and reach them easily.

- Roll, don't fold, stored carpets—preferably around a wood or cardboard core. Then wrap them in sheets of plastic or wrapping paper for dust protection.

- Cover furniture and mattresses with wrapping paper or old sheets. Never store mattresses flat; use 4-by-8-inch plywood as dividers to help them stay vertical, standing on their narrow sides.

- If, for any reason, it is not possible to attach shelves to the wall, use freestanding steel shelving (from a home center or an office-supply mail-order catalog). It's often available with casters for mobility.

A slab of wood, two wooden trestles, open shelves and a tabletop unit containing nine tiny cubbyholes add up to an attic corner (above) that would be the envy of anyone seeking a spot to do crafts or any kind of project on their own.

Sized for storing small garments as well as old letters and documents, these sturdy boxes (top and above) can be color-coded to suit your storage needs—effective as long as you post the code where everyone in your household can read it. Or you can simply choose the colors that please you and then note the containers' contents on each chrome label holder.

ATTIC ADVICE

Even with good ventilation and roof fans that switch on and off automatically, attics can build up damaging—and often dangerous—heat, so avoid short- or long-term storage of these items:

- Candles and anything else made of wax
- Combustible items, such as gasoline, kerosene, lighting fluid, motor-oil, paint, paint thinner and propane gas
- Cosmetics, including children's costume makeup
- Film, photography and photo albums
- Packaged foods
- Old phonograph records
- Wool blankets and clothing

- Avoid "mystery boxes" that tend to clutter an attic because no one recalls what's in them. Keep an inventory of everything you store in your attic so you always know what you have on hand.

- Using an indelible marking pen, print in block letters on the top and sides of each container; taped-on labels may peel off over time.

- Be sure your labeling includes the total contents of each container. You don't want to have to open every box to see exactly what's packed inside.

- Color-coordinate your labeling: red or green for Christmas ornaments, blue or pink for baby clothes, for example.

- To make sure your labeling system can be quickly understood, post your color code in a highly visible spot just inside the attic entrance, so anyone searching for a particular item will know where to start.

WEEDING OUT. To make sure you store only what you really do plan to use and need to keep, carefully edit out superfluous items before you pack up and tuck anything away.

- Be ruthless when editing. Look at everything you plan to store in your attic as though through the eyes of a stranger, asking yourself repeatedly, "Do I really need to keep this?"

- Inspect your attic at least twice a year; that way, you'll know where everything is and can dispose of whatever you no longer need.

- To simplify the inspection process, keep and update itemized lists of the contents of each shelf or container stored in your attic.

THE UNINVITING UNDERGROUND

Basements are great catchall spaces, ideal for housing water heaters, heating and cooling systems, home laundries and mini-workshops. Some basements are insulated and paneled, useful as children's playrooms, family rec rooms or as the only spot in a home suitable for bringing in a pool table or holding table-tennis tournaments. But many a basement is simply raw space, with rough concrete walls and floors. Basically uninviting, this underground afterthought gets little attention—except from those family members who use it to store boxes packed with stuff they probably don't need but cannot bear to part with.

- To know for certain what your basement holds, before attempting to organize, remove everything from cartons, boxes, cabinets, shelving and drawers.

- Spread all your stored items out on the basement floor. This will make it easier for you to take a complete inventory.

- Separate everything into stacks or piles labeled "Keep," "Give away" and "Toss."

- Don't keep anything you no longer need or haven't used or thought about in at least three years. Be as hard-nosed here as you were in sifting through the contents of your attic; the same rules apply.

- Keep in mind that items you forgot you actually had should be the first ones to consider getting rid of.

- Evaluate each of the items you decide to keep, asking yourself if it really belongs in the basement. Perhaps it should be stored closer to where you are likely to need it—in or near the bathroom, kitchen or pantry, for example—so it can be retrieved quickly and easily.

- Cluster similar items together, then label or color-code the boxes and tack a map or locator chart to the wall. The next time you plan to entertain, you'll know where to find that giant turkey platter or the pasta pot you only need when Little Leaguers come for dinner.

- When storing wine here, select the darkest corner of the basement and lay each bottle on its side—so the corks stay wet.

- Improvise a wine rack, if necessary, by obtaining a sturdy carton (with dividers) from a liquor store or wine merchant. Turn the carton on its side and attach a label so you know what you have.

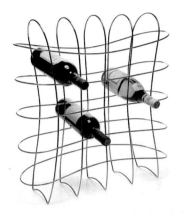

With the whimsical appeal of a whirligig, this portable rack (top) can go wherever you choose to keep your wine. Made of stainless steel with a chrome finish, it holds up to 20 bottles, all stored at just the right angle. A wooden rack, with four large compartments set at an angle (above), is a more conventional way for a wine collection to be stored.

A handsome system for keeping tools and garden gear orderly in a finished basement (above), this unit includes cupboards and drawers, adjustable wire shelving and a custom hook arrangement that will allow you to hang tools and implements in the most organized way. Base cabinets are topped with a hardy work surface for doing carpentry projects or potting plants.

VISIBILITY AND ACCESS. One aid to organizing for high-visibility storage in a basement is using cupboards or drawer units on wheels or casters. Ideal for seasonal storage, these pieces can be rolled near the foot of the stairs when the season approaches—summertime or Christmas, for example—then rolled back when the season ends. Here are some other ideas:

- Upgrade basement lighting. You can make your basement cheerier and, at the same time, expose crannies and corners suitable for storage that might be overlooked otherwise.

- Augment basement lighting by plugging your light sockets into the ends of well-insulated extension cords fastened to ceiling joists. The effect is more practical than pretty, but it's one good way to get the job done.

- Make sure you can see everything you store, but don't leave anything exposed or uncovered. Stackable transparent plastic or acrylic containers are inexpensive home-center purchases, but any sealed container—wood, metal or glass as well as plastic—will be suitable as long as you label its contents.

- Don't store books, old papers or clothing unless your basement is super-dry. Dampness invariably invites mold and mildew.

- Stack firewood outdoors, placed under a waterproof tarpaulin. Stored indoors, in a basement, the wood introduces the possibility of an insect invasion.

- Store solvents, fertilizers and insecticides in a detached garage or outdoors in a waterproof bin, but never in a basement. No matter how tightly lidded your storage containers are, these chemicals may emit noxious odors, thus should not be stored inside your home.

PRACTICAL MATTERS. Except in dry climates, basements are below-ground spaces that collect moisture—condensation that inevitably penetrates concrete walls and floors. Waterproof paint formulated specifically for basements can create a viable moisture barrier. An even more effective, though much more costly, dampness deterrent would be to lay down new flooring that's made of waterproof concrete.

- As a general rule, restrict basement storage to items such as wine that you would prefer to keep cool.

- Another general rule is to try to keep everything off the floor. Even if your storage containers are solid and thoroughly sealed, a heavy rainfall may result in some moisture accumulation seeping into your basement.

- Rest storage containers or freestanding shelf units on sleepers—2-by-4's laid so there is some air space between the floor, which might be damp periodically, and whatever you store. These sleepers will keep some moisture from reaching your goods.

- If your basement is consistently damp, however, consider installing a thermostatically controlled electric dehumidifier to dry it out.

- Arrange your storage from the outside in—longterm storage along peripheral walls, items of seasonal interest right in the center.

- Don't overlook your basement stairs. The space directly under them can be harnessed for shelving, cabinetry or any kind of built-in or freestanding storage unit.

- Make the most of overhead space. Hanging shelves, which you can suspend from ceiling joists, can be fashioned from scrap wood or purchased precut at a home center or lumberyard.

Weatherproof, heavy-duty plastic recycling bins (above) can be lifted on and off this wheeled cart by gripping the handles at each end. Having wheels reduces heavy lifting; you can roll your recyclables to where they need to go. Rust- and chip-proof toolboxes (below) can tolerate abuse and neglect. They come in two sizes and can be latched tight for security and carried around by their handles.

UP AND DOWN BONUSES

Drawers, wine storage and cabinets in custom shapes and sizes (above) make use of every inch of space under stairs leading down to a basement. Another under-stair alternative is this classy home office (below), with desk and cupboard spaces, a row of cubbies for mail and bills, plus open shelving and an overhead cabinet for hiding as well as displaying special items.

UNDER-STAIR STORAGE

That open space beneath the stairs leading to an attic or other upstairs rooms or down to your basement is like a golden triangle—a great place for built-in storage or for freestanding units you can tuck in place. Whether you choose open shelving, drawer units or closed cupboards, under-stair storage can be a space-saving convenience. It also makes the stairway multifunctional, an enhancement of a home's interior architecture. Store items there that you may need in a hurry, even if you won't need them often. Having them there, right under the stairs, means you won't have to explore the entire basement to locate a seasonal essential.

- Consider closed storage—cupboards or drawer units—if there is room to tuck them into your under-stair space. Particularly where basements and attics are concerned, dust accumulates quickly; closed storage ensures that what you store won't be soiled when you're ready to use it.

- Build shelving to fit under the stairs or, if the steps are wide enough, to line the stairs themselves. You can stack items you've sealed in labeled containers, or display decorative objects you rarely use but would enjoy putting on display.

- Use that under-stair "golden triangle" as a place to set up a home office. There should be plenty of room for a desk or work surface with cupboards and drawers underneath. Good lighting plus phone and computer access would be important complements, but make sure there are nearby outlets before you bring in furnishings.

Shelving that lines one side of a stairway (left) takes little pedestrian space but offers bonus storage for a variety of objects. Note that these custom-made shelf units frame a window and continue on to the house's first floor. Here's another attempt to make the most of a walkout basement (below). There is a large niche with open shelving, and a vent-free gas fireplace, which means that this finished basement can serve as a relaxing retreat year-round.

8 EXTERIOR EXTRAS

SPACES THAT ARE PART OF YOUR HOME, though somewhat removed from its core, are often the likeliest clutter magnets. You don't live in your garage, tool shed, workshop or garden shed, for example, but you may well overuse each of them for storage.

The garage, created to shelter the family car, long ago became shared space. Whether built to hold one, two or three vehicles, it has inevitably become a nesting place for athletic gear, carpentry and garden tools. Organized well, a garage can absorb all these elements and still leave room enough for cars. Separate home workshops and garden sheds have taken some of the onus off of the traditional garage, but keeping these ancillary spaces orderly can be even more challenging because of their relatively small size. Always keep in mind that each of these spaces represents a *structure*, and as such deserves thoughtful consideration.

This gardener's worktable (opposite), by Doyle Builders in Princeton, New Jersey, was designed specifically to tuck into a small space. Crafted of cedar, it has one sturdy shelf, with generous storage space directly under it, topped by a 22-by-51-inch work surface.

JOURNAL JOTTINGS

"The number-one challenge in organizing a garage is deciding how to arrange what you store there," says Ace's Helpful Hardware Man Lou Manfredini. *"It might be helpful to create a journal about the way you plan to utilize the space. Jot down on a piece of paper: 'I've got to keep the lawnmower there, and I want space for my wheelbarrow, because I do a lot of gardening, and I'd love to have an area where I can pop some plants. Also, I've got an old refrigerator that goes in there and I need to store cases of soda.' You have to identify how you want to use your garage and establish that before you invest in any storage system."*

Arranged specifically to fit this garage, these storage units (right)—some on wheels, some hung from a wall system—have steel fronts, and the closed cabinets have large, easily gripped handles. Topped with a thick wooden slab, a trio of units can become the base of a worktable when pulled close together.

THE CLUTTERED GARAGE. Like an overgrown closet, the garage holds and hides an assortment of items. It's a warehouse for toys, tools, athletic equipment, patio and deck furniture, papers and recyclables and even old clothes—along with one or more cars, of course. What is useful and needed often gets buried under gear that should have been disposed of long ago. Help is at hand, however. Here are some practical ways to turn your garage into a neat, superefficient, storage facility:

- Back your vehicles out of the garage and remove everything else—the items hanging from overhead beams, the stuff packed inside cabinets and drawers, the dusty cartons shoved onto shelving and pushed into dark corners.

- Sweep your empty garage thoroughly, probing every corner and cranny; then hose off the floor. When dry, inspect to make sure the floor is truly clean.

- To remove stubborn grime, grease spots and oil stains, dip a stiff-bristled, long-handled brush into a bucket containing one part detergent mixed with one part hot water; then vigorously scrub the garage floor.

- After your cleanup, fill any cracks you find with all-purpose urethane grout. If the cracks are sizable, use a mortar compound that you can find at your nearest lumberyard or home center.

- If your garage floor needs protection against future spills and stains, use a long-handled brush to apply one coat of sealer or two coats of industrial epoxy paint.

- Make sure the floor is dry before applying sealer or paint; then let it dry completely afterward before replacing items to be stored.

- Don't put anything back until you have examined each item.

THE WEEDING-OUT PROCESS. It's the most arduous challenge, one you must deal with before doing anything else. "The first step is to do a quick run-through, pulling out all the stuff you can lose," advises Barry J. Izsak, former president of the National Association of Professional Organizers. "It is a pre-purge or pre-sort, as it gives you a chance to get rid of dried-up paint, broken tools and the old baby stroller." These are easy decisions, of course, and he suggests you start making them the moment you start emptying the garage. Put like items together so you'll have an easier time editing.

Epoxy-coated steel, in a mesh configuration, is used to create the wall-hung shelves and the drawers on wheels that comprise this highly flexible garage storage system (above). Mesh surfaces prevent dust from accumulating, and the ultratight weave means that tiny items are less likely to fall through.

Garage storage with a Swedish flair: this system (right) includes rails, hooks and generous open shelving in classic white birch. Boxes, baskets, bins and other accessories are available to make the most of every usable storage space.

LOOK UP!

"The more vertical space you can utilize, the more you can get into your garage," notes Lou Manfredini, Ace Hardware's Helpful Hardware Man.

COEXISTING WITH CARS. After determining what to keep, what to toss and what to give away, you need to decide how to store what you retain. This challenge involves arranging things skillfully. If you live in a temperate climate and are content to park your vehicles in the driveway, your problems are few. The garage can become a kind of home storage vault filled with tools, garden gear and endless purchases from bulk-sale discount retailers. If you are intent on storing your cars as well as your goods, however, you must become a clever space planner, utilizing every available expanse of wall, plus whatever room you have overhead.

- To make garage storage more efficient, add more lighting so that everything you keep there can be seen.

- Before shopping for storage aids, measure your garage and catalog its contents, so you will know exactly what you need and can be sure that everything fits.

124

- Check out mail-order catalogs, the Internet or your nearest home center to find the cabinets and compartmentalized shelf systems that are large enough to hold all your gear and also fit into your available storage space.

- Keep as much as possible of what you store off the floor. Whether you hammer long nails to the wall or screw in vinyl-covered hooks, make sure you hang, rather than lean, such items as garden tools, axes, even power tools.

- If you store things in cardboard cartons, keep them off the floor by resting them on bricks or blocks of pressure-treated wood. This way, they are less likely to be damaged, should any dampness seep into the garage, and will be safely out of the way next time you sweep the garage floor.

- Hang ladders sideways, on hooks or brackets, or store them flat overhead on ceiling rafters.

- To expand your garage's storage capacity, hang a cabinet from hooks attached to cleats on the back wall. Or, suspend shelving from the rafters or ceiling.

- Utilize whatever space is open above the front of your vehicles: Suspend a cabinet or shelf unit from rafters or the inside roof, but make sure you leave room for your garage door, if it is one that swings up or slides overhead on tracks.

- To stow large items, opt for galvanized-steel or heavy-duty plastic containers. You can stand garden tools in them or, if they have lids, use the containers to protect bags of lawn seed or bird food from bugs and rodents.

- Make hand tools and gardening implements more accessible by hanging them from nails or hooks on Peg-Board. (To make sure each tool has its place—and goes back there after use—consider painting silhouettes on the Peg-Board surface.) You can also group like items in metal or plastic buckets hung from hooks or nails.

- Place small items—nails, nuts and bolts, for example—in clear glass jars on eye-level shelves. Or, group like items in small, sealable plastic bags nailed to the wall. You tend to forget about things that are kept out of sight.

- Reuse discarded items for storage: old drawer cabinets or file drawers for building supplies, a shoe bag hung on the wall to hold small garden tools, perhaps a hammock stretched across the rear of the garage strictly for sports gear.

You may need a ladder to reach what you store (top), but this acrylic-coated steel unit can be suspended right over the hood of your car. You probably won't want to use this floating shelf for items you need to get at often, but whatever you keep here will always be visible. Wire shelving attached to the garage wall (above) can be mounted low to the floor or as high as you can reach. Different drawer and shelf sizes let you create a system that responds to all of your garage storage needs.

GARAGE STORAGE SAVVY. Some people want everything to be kept visible; others prefer packaging what they store, whether it is in wood or metal containers or sensibly arranged in bins or drawers. "You have to be aware of how you want things stored before you put anything back in your garage," says Barry Izsak. "Once you do put things back, be sure to label the container, label the shelf, label the drawer. Commit to doing this; tweak the system if necessary, but be sure to maintain it."

- Arrange garage contents by need: Place what you use often where you can get to it easily—at eye level, near the front of the garage or close to the door.

- Deal with big items first: lawn mower, leaf blower, pole-hole driver. Place them where you can retrieve them easily, then build the rest of your storage scheme around them.

- Relegate seasonal items to distant corners or the upper reaches of the garage, stretched across the rafters.

- Note the environment of the area you live in. If your climate is often either hot and humid or cold and damp, avoid wood shelving. It may rot, warp or crack when exposed to dampness overtime.

- Because garage temperatures fluctuate widely, avoid storing such perishable items as films, photos or audiotapes there.

- Don't overload your shelves. As all shelving, as well as hooks, is sold with a predetermined weight limit, be sure you know that limit before you finalize your purchases.

- Consider safety when you store; carefully secure drills, axes and other heavy tools. Avoid using freestanding shelves that climbing children can pull or knock over.

- Keep the heaviest items— tool chests and building materials—plus paints and fluids such as antifreeze on lower areas of heavy-duty shelves fastened to the exposed wall studs.

- Hang bicycles, backpacks, folding chairs, garden hoses, tire rims and other bulky items from ceiling beams or joists. You can find large-scale vinyl- or rubber-coated ladder hooks for this purpose at hardware stores or home centers.

- To optimize the limited space your garage may offer, consider installing a custom storage system—with shelves, bins or drawer units sized to suit your needs and space. For sources, shop the Internet or your nearest home center.

Two bikes can be stored capably on a gravity bike rack (opposite, top) that leans just 19 inches out from a wall. Its steel-tubing frame has an epoxy-coated black finish. A golf organizer with a grained-wood finish (opposite, bottom) has a carpeted compartment for a golf bag plus shelves for shoes, hats and gloves. A wall system for sports gear (left) has open shelves, sturdy hooks and wide brackets. Plus, there is edged shelving, to keep golf balls and roller skates from rolling off.

SAFE KEEPING

To make your garage a safe place for storage:

- Keep paints, toxic chemicals, pesticides and flammable liquids in their original containers and away from a heat source—preferably in a locked cabinet out of the reach of children.

- Store gasoline and propane gas tanks in well-ventilated areas.

- Do not keep old car batteries or batteries of any kind. Over time, they can leak and possibly explode.

- Do not dump batteries in the trash. Vehicle batteries can be exchanged when new ones are purchased, but you are personally responsible for both wet- and dry-cell battery disposal. Contact Battery Solutions, Inc., at 800-852-8127 or www.batteryrecycling.com. To dispose specifically of power-tool, camcorder, digital-camera, cordless and cell-phone batteries in a safe, environmentally sound way, go to www.rbrc.org to find a collection site near you.

SHED AND WORKSHOP CHALLENGES

"Like a cook who must keep her kitchen clean, a gardener needs to keep tools organized," says Deb Soule, owner of Avena Botanicals in Rockport, Maine. In truth, a garden shed may start out as a place to store fertilizer and lawn seed as well as tools, but all too often it becomes a receptacle for items that have no place being there, crowding the items it should contain. By clearing out and cleaning the shed, you're likely to turn up things you thought long lost.

GETTING STARTED. Remove everything from shed shelves and floor, sorting as you go. Plan to get rid of what you know you will never use; place disposable items in a separate pile. Next, clean the interior walls and floor, using scrub brushes, heavy-duty sponges and liquid household cleaner in a warm-water solution. Don't bring in storage accessories until the shed is completely dry. Before putting anything back, plan where and how to store all those items you're determined to keep.

Compact but capacious, this vertical storage shed (above) is 6½ feet tall but takes up only 12 square feet of ground space. It's made of blow-molded resin, which makes it sturdy as well as lightweight. This back porch (right) was transformed into an indoor garden room with whitewashed wall paneling, a Peg-Board-backed metal shelf unit, to hold hand tools and containers, plus a trellis with hooks, so you can hang whatever you wish.

- Consider visibility when deciding how to organize your shed. What cannot be seen may never be used.

- Find places for additional shelving. If your shed has exposed studs, you can cut scrap 1-by-3-inch lumber into shelves to mount between the vertical members.

- To make the most of shelves built between exposed studs, create door panels with Peg-Board cut to fit each section of shelving. Attach piano hinges to these panels, and you'll have closed-cabinet storage plus visible storage in front of it. Using Peg-Board hooks, you can hang small tools on each door front; reserve the shelving inside for storing seed packets and other small objects.

- Consider mounting shelves on the inside of the shed door itself, and hang your most-used small tools there on hooks.

- Hang long-handled tools on shed walls with hooks or nails.

- As an alternative, use one or more spaces between studs for long-handled tool storage. To do this safely, attach a strip of 1-by-2-inch strapping lumber to a pair of studs at both knee and waist height to keep the tools from falling over.

- Another alternative would be to cut off the tops and bottoms of any size tin cans, taking care to cut away and file down jagged edges. Nail the cans at waist height vertically to the walls or studs to create a spot in which to stand each tall tool.

- If your shed lacks a potting bench, an ideal surface for tackling messy jobs, plan to build one if you have room. It will provide a work surface on top and storage space underneath.

- If your shed is well ventilated, feel free to store paint remover, oil, gasoline and cleaning solvents there, but keep in mind that paint should be kept where temperature fluctuations are minimal.

- Be moisture-conscious: Keep what you plan to store off the floor. Whether it's made of wood, steel, concrete or raw earth, a shed floor cannot resist dampness.

- Arrange to put your collection of weed killers and insecticides out of the reach of young children. Keep these products in lockable storage, or put a padlock on the shed door.

Depending on the kind and number of garden tools you own, here are three different ways to consider storing them. First is a wall-hung bracket (top) that gets the most out of small space. Second is a wall-wide 16-pocket garden tool organizer (above, center) made of durable poly-mesh. Next is a Peg-Board storage wall (above) that tucks under a shelf in a garden shed.

ORGANIZING AIDS. When the shed is clean and dry, you're ready to put its contents back inside. Start with the largest items: power mower, leaf blower and wheelbarrow; place them where they can be rolled out handily.

■ Store sacks of fertilizer, peat moss and mulch in super-size trash containers or on skids to keep them off the floor or the ground. Or, improvise skids by laying chunks of scrap lumber on stacked bricks or blocks of scrap 2-by-4's.

■ Stack flowerpots by size; keep in mind that terra-cotta pots may not stack well. Separating them with old rags or sheets of newspaper or wax paper will make the stacks easier to pull apart when needed.

■ Use a bucket that you can hang by its handle or set on a shelf as a compact catchall for small tools and other loose items that are often lost or overlooked.

Here's a garden tool organizer on wheels (above) that holds a lot. It has rack space for tall items, and pockets in its canvas sides for small tools as well as gloves. And the beauty is that it can be rolled wherever you need to work. This lockable all-pine garden shed (right) is available by mail order and shipped disassembled. It has a weather-resistant asphalt roof plus two roomy interior shelf units. Hardly more than 5 feet tall, it will store all your garden and pool supplies in a 31-by-60 inch space.

PAINT POINTERS

- Buy only as much paint as you need to get a particular job done. No matter how carefully you seal the can, leftover paint can deteriorate over time.

- When buying paint, obtain a sample chip and attach it to a card with the name and number of the color. Use the card for reference when you need to reorder paint for touch-ups.

- If you do have small amounts of leftover paint, transfer it from the can to a glass jar or wide-mouth plastic container. Label the container, and dab the label with paint so you will know what color you have.

- Never toss half-empty paint cans in the trash. As with solvents, oils, insecticides and cordless-tool batteries, it behooves you to handle old paint with care. Call town hall or your local sanitation department to find out when your local trash-collecting facility schedules hazardous-waste pickup and disposal.

Made of lightweight resin, this garden shed (above) is big enough to hold a full-size tractor—with front and rear doors for easy access, two skylights guaranteed not to leak plus optional shelf and tool-rack accessories that can be attached to interior walls without nails, bolts or screws. All of this sits on a footprint measuring 7 by 10½ feet.

If all your garden gear invariably lands on the deck, this corner deck box (above, left) may suit your style. Closed up, it's self-contained under its own roof. Pulled open, it has slots for tools and shelves for fertilizers and pots. Heavy-duty self-stick hooks and spring clips (above) enable you to expand the storage capacity of any garden worktable so that hand tools, seed packets, gloves and even a tin bucket can be hung in plain sight.

These two workshop organizers are built to stand the tests of time and use. Both are made of commercial-grade heavy-gauge steel, with a particleboard surface for each shelf. The workbench has two half-width drawers plus a Peg-Board back for hanging tools and other essentials. The shelf unit has five adjustable shelves; each can hold up to 1,000 pounds.

END WORKSHOP CLUTTER. Most homes have a supply of tools stashed away—sometimes in a kitchen drawer, sometimes in a steel box, but often in a separate workshop or work area. That space may be so messy and chaotic that it's hard to find tools when you need them. Having a place reserved for home and garden projects would be a plus, but only if organized well and kept clutter-free.

- Inventory what you own. If you have duplicate tools of the same size and weight, consider giving away those of lesser quality or with greater wear. Retain only the best ones.

- When shopping for nails, screws and other hardware, resist the urge to buy economy-size packages. Acquire only as much as you think you need to complete a particular project.

- When using nails, tacks or any small packaged items, remove only what you need, then reseal the labeled package with masking tape. Always know the size and nature of the items you have on hand, that's an easy way to stay organized.

KEEPING TRACK OF TOOLS. The key to doing just that involves storage organization. "Group everything," advises Joe Carter, a seasoned woodworker, general contractor and a former senior editor of *This Old House* magazine. "Keep garden tools and work tools separate—when you come looking for the lawn edger, it'll be where it's supposed to be, not hidden behind a handsaw."

- To play it safe and also save precious time and energy, do a rough plan so you'll know in advance where all your gear should go.

- Keep everything off the floor. All metal tools and power tools should be stored in a dry area to prevent rust.

- Arrange tools according to how often you use them. What you need regularly should be stored at eye level, where it can be spotted and accessed easily.

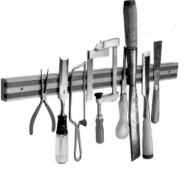

Everything from paint to power tools can be stored on the four shelves (three are adjustable) of this lockable steel cabinet (top). Twenty-four inches of solid wood with magnetic implants make the wall-hung tool holder (above) a flexible storage instrument. A high-concept storage ensemble (left) has base and wall cabinets and panel-hung hard plastic shelving.

- If you have wall space, consider mounting Peg-Board behind your work area to hang tools on. Available at lumberyards and home centers, Peg-Board comes in 4-by-8-foot sheets and can be cut to fit specific space needs with a handsaw.

- To make the most of your Peg-Board, and have tools where you can always locate them, draw or paint an outline so it's clear that each tool has its own storage spot.

- Make workshop shelving shallow. Anything stored on too-deep shelves is likely to be buried and become unreachable.

Pieces of self-stick adhesive ease the chore of neatening a workshop (above). With dividers in each of four drawers, to inspire further organizing efforts, this storage chest (below) can be mounted on a wall or kept on a shelf. As an aid to customizing your own space, a workshop kit (below, right) provides hooks, racks and trays.

STORAGE AS AN ART. Whether your focus is a workshop, garage or garden shed, the key to decluttering each and any of these spaces can be found in the way you organize what they contain. If, let's say, your garage is truly a catchall space, be sure not to only keep your lawn and garden equipment separate from home repair tools, but also keep auto-repair gear apart from sports equipment.

The next step is to be sure you make the most of whatever storage space you have. For example: "Use rafters to store lengths of pipe and lumber," suggests Lester R. Walker, a Woodstock, New York, architect. This would also be a good place to store sheets of plywood plus other building supplies you may not use very often. Here are other practical ideas:

- Be sure you always utilize the space beneath your worktable. Fill it with two- or three-drawer metal cabinets or low file cabinets (usually available at flea markets and second-hand office furniture stores). Label each drawer so you'll know what it contains without having to open it.

- Buy inexpensive plastic or rubberized dish-wash basins in which to store small items. Two or three of these basins, aligned on open shelving, should hold most essentials, as long as they're kept in properly labeled boxes.

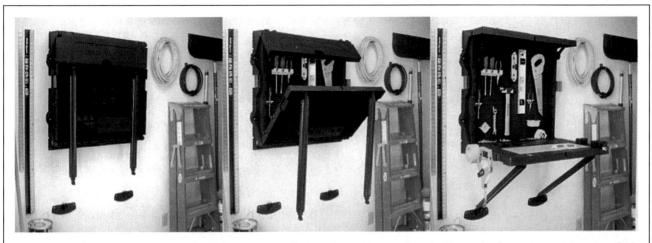

- Store nails, screws, nuts and washers in small glass jars. Fasten the lids to the underside of wood shelving; unscrew a jar when you need its contents.

- Use transparent storage where possible, so you can always see what you've got. Mason jars or plastic containers make contents visible and lessen the need for detailed labeling.

- Reuse clean, empty coffee cans to store small hand tools and clean paintbrushes (bristles up). Place the cans on shelves or nail firmly to the solid walls or posts behind or beside your worktable.

- Give new life to old chests, file cabinets and kitchen cabinet units unless they are serviceable enough to be sold or shared. Bring them to your work area for tool storage.

- Avoid "snake-pit" storage; don't toss loose extension cords into a drawer—you'll never find the one you want when you need it. Using a wall-mounted bracket, or even a garden-hose holder, would be an excellent way to keep cords visible—and separate.

- Store small power tools and their accessories in clear plastic bags, so you can see what you own. It may also be wise to tack plastic bags to the wall, keeping them off your worktable.

Shown in three phases (above), a fold-down, wall-hung workstation goes from flat and unobtrusive to open and functional, presenting a usable work surface beneath the stored tools.

DONATING INSIGHTS

DISPOSING OF WHAT YOU NO LONGER NEED means making a decision: Are the items in question serviceable, the clothing wearable? If not, you will have to find a way to trash them. In weeding out all of the surplus possessions your household has accumulated, you will find a great many items you no longer need, use or wear. If they cannot be passed on to someone in your family, they can be donated to any of a number of charitable organizations, each of which should be able to supply a form enabling you to credit the donation on your next tax return.

What to donate? "Serviceable" means clean clothing; blankets and towels without holes or tears; books without cracked bindings or missing pages; gadgetry that still works. (No charity is equipped to do finite repair jobs.) Local religious organizations may have outreach programs for disadvantaged residents, and you will find that homeless shelters, retreats for battered women, senior centers and children's hospitals will all welcome whatever usable surplus is salvaged from your home.

Here are specific suggestions:

- **BOOKS AND MAGAZINES:** Query the public library, your nearest hospital, nursing home, rehabilitation facility or senior center.

- **CLOTHING, FURNITURE, BRIC-A-BRAC:** If no local charity is interested, get in touch with Goodwill Industries International (www.goodwill.org) or Salvation Army (www.salvationarmyusa.org) to locate the nearest outlet.

- **ELECTRONIC EQUIPMENT:** If they're in good working order, donate computers, printers, cameras and music systems to Share the Technology (www.sharetechnology,org); reusable cellphones to The Wireless Foundation (www.wirelessfoundation.org).

- **EYEGLASSES:** Donate to the Lions Club's nationwide eyeglass recycling program (www.lionsclubs.org).

- **MUSICAL INSTRUMENTS:** If a local school is not interested, contact Music Go Round (www.musicgoround.com), which may be willing to buy or trade the items.

- **SPORTS GEAR AND EQUIPMENT:** If no school is interested, contact Play It Again Sports (www.playitagainsports.com); they may be prepared to purchase or trade equipment you no longer need.

BATTERY SAVVY
It is illegal to dump batteries of any kind in the trash. Vehicle batteries can be exchanged when new ones are purchased, but you are responsible for disposing of both wet- and dry-cell batteries. Contact Battery Recycling, Inc. (www.BatteryRecycling.com), at 800-852-8127 .

ORGANIZING HELP

PEOPLE

JOHN A. BUSCARELLO, ASID
212-691-5881
www.buscarello.com

CAROL WEISSMAN INTERIOR DESIGN
913-897-6520

JAMIE DRAKE, ASID
212-754-3099
www.drakedesignassociates.com

GAIL GREEN, ASID
212-906-0110
www.greenandcompanydesign.com

BARRY J. IZSAK
512-419-7526
www.arrangeitall.com

LOREN REID SEAMAN & ASSOCIATES
847-550-6363
www.lrsdesigns-decorating.com

HEATHER MOE
South Pacific Kitchen & Construction, Inc.
858-459-9086
www.southpacifickitchenandcon.com

JEROME CURRIE HANAUER & ASSOCIATES
917-446-5158

THE MONEY PIT
www.888moneypit.com

NATIONAL ASSOCIATION OF PROFESSIONAL ORGANIZERS
847-375-4746
www.napo.net

NEAL ZIMMERMAN & ASSOCIATES, AIA
860-561-5756
www.atworkathome.com

RENT-A-HUSBAND
877-994-8229
www.rentahusband.com

RODERICK N. SHADE INTERIOR DESIGN
212-865-7816
www.roderickshade.com

SHELLEY MORRIS INTERIOR DESIGN
914-764-5130

DONNA SMALLIN
Organizing Plain & Simple Monthly
www.unclutter.com

BILL WEST
866-842-7243
www.garagez.com

MARK T. WHITE, CKD
Kitchen Encounters
410-263-4900
www.kitchenencounters.biz

SUPPLIES & FURNITURE

ACE HARDWARE
866-2290-5334
www.acehardware.com

ARISTOKRAFT, INC.
812-482-2527
www.Aristokraft.com

BROOKSTONE
800-846-3000
www.brookstone.com

THE COMPANY STORE
800-323-8000
www.the companystore.com

THE CONTAINER STORE
800-786-7315
www.containerstore.com

CRATE & BARREL
800-237-5672
www.crateandbarrel.com

ELFA
201-777-11554
www.elfa.com

FREEDOM RAIL
800-210-7712
www.organizes-it.com

FRONTGATE
888-263-9850
www.frontgate.com

GARAGETEK
866-664-2724
www.garagetek.com

GARDENERS EDEN
800-822-1214
www.gardenerseden.com

GET ORGANIZED
800-803-9400
www.shopgetorganized.com

GLADIATOR GARAGEWORKS
by Whirlpool Corporation
866-342-4089

GRANDIN ROAD
888-263-9850
www.frontgate.com

HARD-TO-FIND TOOLS
800-926-7000
www.brookstone.com

HOLD EVERYTHING
800-421-2264
www.holdeverything.com

THE HOME DEPOT
800-553-3199
www.homedepot.com

HOME TRENDS
800-810-2340
www.shophometrends.com

IKEA
800-434-4532
www.ikea.com

JOHN DEERE
800-544-2122
www.johndeeregifts.com

LEE VALLEY TOOLS
800-267-8735
www.leevalley.com

LEVENGER
800-667-8034
www.levenger.com

LILLIAN VERNON
800-901-9402
www.lillianvernon.com

LOWE'S
800-445-6937
www.lowes.com

OFFICE MAX
800-283-7674
www.officemax.com

ORGANIZE EVERYTHING
800-600-9817
www.organize-everything.com

PIER 1 IMPORTS
800-245-4595
www.pier1.com

POLIFORM USA
888-765-4367
www.poliformusa.com

POTTERY BARN
800-922-5507
www.potterybarn.com

RELIABLE HOME OFFICE
800-733-6959
www.reliablehomeoffice.com

REV-A-SHELF
800-857-8721
www.revashelf.net

RUBBERMAID HOME PRODUCTS
888-895-2110
www.rubbermaid.com

SAUDER WOODWORKING
800-523.3987
www.sauder.com

CLOSETS

SCHULTE DISTINCTIVE STORAGE
800-669-3225
www.schultestorage.com

SMITH & HAWKEN
800-940-9817
www.smithandhawken.com

STACKS AND STACKS
800-761-5222
www.stacksandstacks.com

THE STANLEY WORKS
800-782-6539
www.stanleyworks.com

THE STORAGE STORE
800-600-9817
www.thestoragestore.com

TAYLOR GIFTS
800-829-1133
www.taylorgifts.com

WALLS+FORMS, INC.
972-980-7320
www.wallsforms.com

3M
800-934-7355
www.commandadhesive.com

CALIFORNIA CLOSETS
800-274-6754
www.calclosets.com

CLOSET FACTORY
800-318-8800
www.closetfactory.com

CLOSETMAID
800-874-0008
www.closetmaid.com

CLOSETS BY DESIGN
800-293-3744
www.closetsbydesign.com

CLOSETS TO GO
888-312-7424
www.closetstogo.com

EASYCLOSETS.COM
800-910-0129
www.easyclosets.com

CREDITS

Front cover: (top left) SPC Custom Publishing, (top right) Alan Kaplanas, (center) Freedom Rail, (bottom left) Charles Schiller, (bottom right) Hold Everything. Front flap: Edmund Barr. Back flap: (top) Jeff McNamara, (bottom) Robin Stubbert. Back cover: (top left) David Duncan Livingston, (center) SieMatic, (bottom left) James Yochum, (bottom right) IKEA.

2: William P. Steele; 8: David Duncan Livingston; 10 (bottom left): Jeff McNamara; 10 (bottom right): Gridley & Graves; 11 (top left): Frontgate; 11 (top right): L.L. Bean; 11 (bottom right): Aimee Herring; 11 (bottom left): Bombay Company; 12 (top): JC Penney; 12 (center): The Container Store; 12 (bottom right): Jessie Walker; 13 (left): Southern Progress Corporation; 13 (right): Polly Wreford/Homes & Gardens UK IPC + Syndication; 14: Kate Roth; 16 (top): Room & Board; 16 (right): Stanley Furniture; 17: Virginia MacDonald; 18: Gridley & Graves; 19 (top): ABC Distributing; 19 (center): Spiegel; 19 (bottom): Edmund Barr; 20: Edmund Barr; 21 (top): Steve McDonald for Crate & Barrel; 21 (bottom): Mark Lohman; 22: David Duncan Livingston; 23 (top): Brian Vanden Brink; 23 (bottom): Robert Pelletier; 24: Claudio Santini; 27: Matthew Millman; 28: Jim Christy; 29: Matthew Millman; 30 (top): James Yochum; 30 (bottom): Philip Wegener; 31: Robin Stubbert; 32 (top): SPC Custom Publishing

"Creative Ideas for Your Home & Garden"; 32 (bottom left): The Container Store; 32 (bottom right): Grandin Road www.grandinroad.com - 800/ 533-7502; 33: Freedom Rail; 34: The Container Store; 35: IKEA; 36: Gridley & Graves; 38 (top): Charles Schiller; 38 (bottom): Steven Randazzo; 39: The Container Store; 40: Alex Hayden; 41 (top): Robin Stubbert; 41 (center): IKEA; 41 (bottom): John Gould Bessler; 42 (top left): KraftMaid; 42 (center): Diamond Cabinets; 42 (bottom left): Knape & Vogt; 42 (top right): Merillat; 42 (bottom right): Gridley & Graves; 43 (top): Diamond Cabinets; 43 (center): Gridley & Graves; 43 (bottom): O'Sullivan; 44 (top left): Design Within Reach; 44 (top right): Jeff McNamara; 44 (bottom): Robin Stubbert; 45 (top left): John Gould Bessler; 45 (top right) Gridley & Graves; 45 (center right): Rev-A-Shelf; 45 (bottom left): Philip Clayton-Thompson; 46 (top): Gridley & Graves; 46 (bottom): SieMatic; 47: Gridley & Graves; 48 (top): Bulthaup; 48 (bottom): Robin Stubbert; 49 (top): IKEA; 49 (center): Mundial; 49 (bottom): Plain & Fancy; 50 (top): Woodmode; 50 (bottom left): John Gould Bessler; 50 (bottom right): Mark Lohman; 51 (top): The Container Store; 51 (bottom): Diamond Cabinets; 54 (top): Jessie Walker; 54 (bottom): Closet Max; 55: John Gould Bessler; 56 (top): Merillat; 56 (bottom): Freedom Rail; 57 (center left): Hold Everything;

ACKNOWLEDGMENTS

The author is grateful to Olivia L. Monjo, Editor in Chief of Woman's Day Special Interest Publications, for conceiving the idea for this book, to Ilana Schweber and Anthi Keeling for making so much of its visual content available, to Doug Schulkind for his eagle-eyed review of the manuscript and to Dorothée Walliser for making this book possible and getting it done on time.

Additional thanks for supplying images must also be extended to: Lorralyn Juergens, Brookstone; Bette Kahn and Joan Perniconi, Crate & Barrel; Kathy Whitney, L.L. Bean; Ron D'Amico and Christine Soner, IKEA; Kate St. Clair, SPC Custom Publishing Marketing (for Lowe's); Carolyn McMannama, The Container Store; Emily Shirden, Sauder; and Jessica Kenderian, Grandin Road.

JUN 07